# From Sartre
## to the
## New Novel

Kennikat Press
# National University Publications
Series in Literary Criticism


*General Editor*
Eugene Goodheart
*Professor of Literature, Massachusetts Institute of Technology*

# *From Sartre*
# *to the*
# *New Novel*

**BETTY T. RAHV**

National University Publications
KENNIKAT PRESS • 1974
Port Washington, N. Y. • London

Library of Congress Catalog Card No. 74-77655
ISBN: 0-8046-9076-6

Manufactured in the United States of America

Published by
Kennikat Press Corp.
Port Washington, N. Y./London

*for William*

# ACKNOWLEDGMENTS

I should like to express a note of gratitude to Robert Champigny for originally inspiring this study and to Eugene Goodheart for genuinely appreciating it. For numerous pertinent suggestions I am indebted to Maureen Gannon, Bernard Elevitch, Richard M. Stevens, S.J., and especially to my colleague Joseph D. Gauthier, S.J., who read the entire manuscript with such a clear critical eye. No less profound is my gratitude to Mathew, Mark, Peter, and above all, Paul, for their patient sustenance along the road to its completion.

# CONTENTS

# CONTENTS *(continued)*

# From Sartre
## to the
## New Novel

# INTRODUCTION

The New Novel in France is patently preoccupied with the question of fictional perspective. The spate of theories accompanying and surrounding the New Novel from its very inception offers ample evidence of this central concern. Each New Novel experiments with fictional techniques which might best convey reality as perceived by a limited subjective consciousness. Point of view thus becomes a paramount issue of the New Novel, linking it once again with the James-Lubbock concept of the art of fiction.[1]

Beginning from the premise that "the art of fiction does not begin until the novelist thinks of his story as a matter to be shown, to be so exhibited that it will tell itself,"[2] James limited fictional perspective to a single character or to several characters in order to avoid intervention of any extrafictional perspective, in particular that of the author. Today, rather than intervention of the author, the New Novel has become all intervention, "intervention du texte dans les textes."[3] James's narrative technique emphasized "scene" over plot and dramatic over narrative modes. Among recent critics of the French novel, John Sturrock finds similarly that "the New Novel is proposing, simply enough, that a fiction should be all scene or representation."[4] What it represents, rather than some sense or reality or meaning beyond its fictional, textual boundaries, is primarily itself. Insisting upon this independent, autonomous character of the New Novel, critics have classified it as a "self-reflective" genre or as an "auto-representation."[5]

Equally akin to the New Novel by virtue of its stress on scene over plot and on the "poetic" over the linear narrative is the notion of "spatial" literature derived from Joyce and first proposed by Joseph Frank in his article of 1945 entitled "Spatial Form in Modern Literature."[6] In this respect, critics as well as authors of the New Novel freely acknowledge their post-Joycean situation. In the New Novel, as in Joyce, pre-occupation with the poetic mode leads to self-consciousness about language. Most recently, for example, Stephen Heath cites both Joycean and Freudian currents as they inform the New Novel's accent on spatial, poetic, and dreamlike forms primarily composing scenes which eclipse linear development of plot and which, because of their multiple language levels, remain open-ended, as in *Finnegans Wake*, long known under the title *Work in Progress.*

*Finnegans Wake* offers the *space* of a work always "in progress," the scene of a play of language and not, as in realist writing, the linear progression of a process of notation. . . . All the "action" takes place, in the circulation through the labyrinthine mesh of languages, on the threshold of sense in the moment of its pro-duction, of the passage from night into day, from the ecstasy of sleep into the wakefulness of speech. . . .[7]

Such spatial literature, which emphasizes scene over plot and dramatic (Lubbock) or poetic (Frank) over narrative modes, addresses itself in the New Novel to the question of its own esthetic. Taking as its point of departure Gide's *mise en abyme,* the New Novel concerns itself solely with the esthetic of the creative act along with all its attendant aspects, such as play within the play, the masks of appearance and reality, and more profoundly, ambiguities in the reflective return of the same eternal themes with variations. In order to allow the reader not only to understand the process of creating but also to engage in the creative act itself, the New Novel revels in ambiguity. Ambiguous at its very core, the New Novel delights in Joycean or even Rabelaisian paradoxes, enigmas, and semantic patterns best described in depth by Johan Huizinga as the profound "ludic" sense underlying all creative endeavor.[8] Critics like Heath sense this ludic quality as a creative challenge:

The terms connected with notions of game and play that Robbe-Grillet today uses almost exclusively to describe his work are expressions of this activity of questioning, contesting, revealing, exploring, demonstrating the limits of, the possibilities of, *playing* with conventional forms.[9]

Others, like Sturrock, clearly link this ludic character of New Novels to the phenomenological "reflective consciousness" which represents the " 'play' in the machine of necessity."[10] Sturrock details more cogently this play element in the contemporary novel as the freedom to rearrange and combine "given" words and images into new fictional patterns. Thus, the author, to weave the given *factual* motifs—images, memories, wishes—into the *fictional* fabric of the New Novel, follows linguistic principles of creativity originally established by Ferdinand de Saussure:

The play of the mind as it is embodied in the *nouveau roman* is constituted by our freedom to rearrange the images or memories of the past without reference to a perceived reality. The images are irreducible facts, the patterns that are made with them are fictions. The relationship between facts and fiction is also paralleled on the linguistic plane. . . . In respect of language as in respect of reality the powers of the mind are truly combinatory and not inventive; we cannot add to the stock of language . . . any more than we can add to the stock of matter.[11]

It is the combining of images, memories, and wishes into patterns, configurations, and juxtapositions—their appearances and disappearances, junctions and disjunctions, iterations and reiterations—which forms the fabric of the New Novel with a view to encompassing as well as instilling a creative challenge.

Essentially a genre preoccupied with creation and creativity, therefore, the New Novel, by questioning its own language and esthetics, continues to play the moral role of avoiding the linguistic pitfalls which surround us, whatever intellectual, propagandistic, or mythological form they may take. Such literature is arduous and demanding in its never-ceasing critical challenge; each new reading opens new horizons at the same time that it challenges the old. Indeed, novelists such as Claude Simon invoke this challenge as a "recreation of our thought," which Sturrock interprets as "revolutionary in the very best sense, being committed to producing a change in the structures of consciousness rather than any direct change in this or that institution or practice."[12] Such an attempt to awaken, reactivate, and reinvigorate the creative consciousness seems indeed to orient the contemporary reader of the New Novel in an opposite direction from that envisaged by the existential phenomenologist of the Sartrean school.

Within the broader phenomenological caste of the New Novel, nevertheless, there emerges a clear esthetic heritage from Sartre, in particular from his literary theories which still tower over those of his followers both sympathetic and antipathetic. Albeit unwittingly, Sartre has played the role of catalyst and mentor to the New Novel. Indeed, Sartre has been denied, chastised, reduced, but never yet entirely eclipsed. Sartre's esthetic notion of the relationship between author, reader and work of art as worked out in the fictional technique of perspective defines most clearly his legacy to the New Novel. The technical handling of person and of tense first proposed by Sartre has evolved in the most creatively meaningful way to give rise to the esthetic formulations of the New Novel in all their variety. In the New Novel Sartre's fictive mask, or *mensonge,* takes over, momentarily leaving aside all commitment, whether political, societal, historical, or other horizontal humanistic considerations in favor of delving into the metaphysical and esthetic vertical plunges of man into himself in order to determine, to revive, and to revivify his creative self, his esthetic dimension. In order to remember, in the platonic tradition of recalling what once was known but must be rediscovered, the emphasis in the New Novel is on rediscovery, on a certain kind of renascence more closely allied to baroque expression and distortion than to Renaissance equilibrium and balance. The components of a single work are interdependent, as are the works of a single author.[13] The same elements recur; each work within the work reflects its esthetic preoccupation, its calling itself into question. By accepting the esthetic challenge of the New Novel, by simply engaging in the act of reading it, the individual reader first calls himself into question, then his world, his creative consciousness, his imagination, and finally his creative relationship to life itself.

The New Novel is therefore more closely allied to Sartrean esthetics than is generally admitted, which demonsrates both its evolution within the phenomenological orientation of this century and its revolution against the committed ethic of the existentialist generation. Rather than consider separately the theories of fiction of the New Novelists which are far from the soundness of Sartre's theoretical writings, this study will consider, within the internal dynamics of a single work of each of three novelists, just how perspective has been worked out in terms of the technical handling of both person and tense, in order to demonstrate the evolution and emergence of the New Novel as a continuation and yet reorientation of Sartre's existential bias in fictional perspective.

# CHAPTER 1

*Il est vain et naïf de posséder sur
le réel un point de vue absolu.*
—Michel Raimond

# SARTRE'S PRECEPTS AND THEIR LITERAL
# APPLICATIONS

Most literary critics of contemporary French fiction agree that 1950 marked the beginning of a genuine upheaval in the novel as a genre in France. At that time it was generally held that the only common denominator shared by New Novelists was their negative attitude toward conventional fictional props, such as plot or character. Numerous predecessors were hailed as foreshadowing the loss of plot or the disappearance of character. Sartre perfectly characterized the new novel by dubbing it *anti-roman*, which remained for many years its popular designation. It was not until quite recently that critics finally began to point toward a more positive esthetic heritage shared by New Novelists.

Although this common esthetic heritage derives in great part from Merleau-Ponty's philosophy of perception, not its least important element is a certain existential bias in fictional perspective, generally overlooked by the majority of critics. This bias stems directly from Sartre. It is my purpose to demonstrate Sartre's pivotal position in developing the esthetic of perspective in the New Novel.

Three important aspects of Sartre's esthetic have had a long-range influence on fictional perspective. All three come from Sartre's existentially informed notion of the relationship between author, reader, and work of art. First as a kind of counterbalance to the traditional self-effacement of the novelist in his work, Sartre strongly urged young novelists to implicate the reader, to "empoigner le lecteur." Secondly, Sartre originally coined the phrase "subjectivités-points-de-vue" as his way of expressing the idea that fictional characters no longer remained objectively observed entities but had become subjectively observing points of view. And last, Sartre held that these "subjectivités-points-de-vue" should express their *prise de conscience*, or contingency, through a series of events which would seem to occur in an ever-unfolding present moment. Such a series of present moments, however handled, should maintain the temporal "ribbon" intact so that the chronology of events could be clearly discerned.

These theoretical notions, particularly with respect to fictional person and time, made a lasting impact on succeeding novelists. Many interpreted him in literal, concrete ways far different from, if not entirely opposite to, Sartre's original intent. In his early literary criticism and theory, Sartre attempted to simplify and to codify fictional perspective; from these same Sartrean *données*, subsequent novelists rendered perspective complex and blatantly ambiguous.

The New Novelists proved particularly adept at cultivating these Sartrean tendencies. Paradoxically, all or nearly all their innovations in perspective came by way of Sartre. In this respect, New Novelists of the fifties and sixties literally followed in the theoretical footsteps of Sartre, but in such a way as to create an entirely opposite kind of novel which maintained from the outset a wholly different rationale. Ideologically, these novelists considered themselves to be revolting against the existential ethic of "committed" literature which followed World War II, but technically, they were quite logically extending certain precepts of the Sartrean esthetic.

## Sartre's theories

Sartre specified the nature and techniques of his esthetic in his early literary criticism of the 1930s and, more definitively, in his theoretical treatise entitled "Qu'est-ce que la Littéra-ture?" of 1947.

First and most conspicuous was his attack on the omni-scient author who interrupts the continuous flow of his story by arbitrarily inserting his presence into his fictional world. In his renowned attack on Mauriac, Sartre clearly stipulated his principle that the author ought to make a studied effort to re-main absent from his fictional world in order for the reader's involvement with the fictional protagonist to be more com-plete. Sartre's theory hinged on two principal points, the first concerning the fictive persona, and the second defining the novel's temporality.

The first point, inherited directly from Flaubert and Joyce, consisted of eliminating insofar as possible overt inter-ventions of the author in his fictional world. Sartre divided authors into two groups: those who remain "inside" their char-acters and those who remain "outside." Vis-à-vis his char-acters, Sartre claimed "le romancier peut être leur témoin ou leur complice, mais jamais les deux à la fois."[1] In reproaching Mauriac for attempting to be both witness and accomplice of Thérèse Desqueyroux, Sartre sought to purify narrative per-spective by rendering it logical and consistent. It was, in fact, because of this very inconsistency of trying both to judge ex-ternally and yet to sympathize internally with his fictional character that many an author had rendered point of view ambiguous and confusing. Mauriac, for example, by cutting into the dialogue of his characters and by summarizing what they were to say, arbitrarily broke into the fictional field of the novel. The reader was at once thrown out of the time-space of the novel while the story was interrupted.

For Sartre, the novel should consist of an unfolding "action" or literary "event" transmitted to the reader through various "subjectivities." The unfolding event itself should supersede and transcend all these subjectivities, yet, in the process, should reveal to each one different aspects of himself. The event exists and has meaning only to the extent that it is meaningful to the fictional characters which it affects. In this respect, each subjectivity, or point of view, is relative, partial, and conjectural, not absolute or omniscient. No objective, or "true," view of the event is to be offered by the author. The novelist's technical problem is to discover and to orchestrate the various subjectivities conscious of the particular event in question; the reader is left to impose his own "absolute reality" on the event, above and beyond these conjectures. Sartre delegated this ultimate esthetic interpretation specifically to the reader in order to limit the author's prerogative to absolute truth and knowledge about his characters. In thus usurping the author's omniscience and handing the reader the last interpretive word, Sartre attempted to balance more evenly the roles of both author and reader vis-à-vis the work of art.

Sartre also reproached authorial omniscience in the name of "freedom" to allow each fictional subjectivity to develop his own consciousness slowly and in familiar surroundings; each story would be one exposing the individual *prise de conscience* rather than one presenting ready-made types with fixed characteristics evident at first appearance and who never altered or changed throughout their story. Such character types resembled "things" in that they "were" but did not "come-to-be": the freedom to choose themselves was denied them. "Seules les choses sont; elles n'ont que des dehors. Les consciences ne sont pas; elles se font."[2]

Sartre considered the introduction of an absolute, or omniscient, point of view into the novel in any guise a double technical error. In the first place, it posited a purely contemplative narrator who observed but who could not be involved in the fictive action; and second, it relegated the story to an absolute plane, atemporal by definition, which allowed its time scheme to be interrupted whenever the writer so desired.

From his initial attempt to eliminate interventions of an omniscient author by limiting perspective to successive points of view relative to a central action, Sartre was led to consider time as inextricably linked to "person" in the determination of fictional perspective.

The second major point that Sartre made with respect to fictional perspective, therefore, stemmed from his concept of temporality in the novel. Sartre considered a certain temporal paradox intrinsic to the novel as a genre. Indeed, the way in which each author in each novel resolved this temporal paradox yielded, for Sartre, the clearest insight into that author's philosophical orientation. Sartre's own philosophical conception of life for any individual as an ever-recurring present moment full of creative potential necessitated a frank duality on the fictional plane. Whereas life's events occur in the present, offering freedom to each individual through a variety of choices, fictional events must be represented as having occurred in the past. Thus, even though the fictional character's choices or actions must be consigned to the past, he must "become" before the reader's very eyes, in a present sense, as his story unfolds. "Dans le roman les jeux ne sont pas faits, car l'homme romanesque est libre. Ils se font sous nos yeux. . . . Le récit, au contraire, se fait au passé."[3]

In discussing the temporal conceptions of Faulkner and Proust, Sartre arrived at a polemical affirmation of the present moment as literarily the most privileged and decisive. Sartre's present moment preempted both the past and the future, but included elements of both. In discussing Proust's time scheme, Sartre wrote, "L'habileté du romancier consiste dans le choix du présent à partir duquel il raconte le passé."[4] With respect to Faulkner's present-moment-sufficient-unto-itself, on the other hand, Sartre declared a future necessary to permit the present moment to be extended or projected; without a future, Faulkner's time severed the present from itself. Sartre's ideal present moment, on the contrary, would never be static or empty, but replete with the past and pregnant with the future.

Sartre's insistence upon the present as the literarily privileged moment perhaps reached its height in his critique of *L'Étranger,* where he went so far as to claim that every sentence, even though written in the *passé composé,* was so encapsulated and self-contained as to convey a present sense.

Thus, he discovered in Camus's style the embodiment of his philosophical orientation:

Toutes les phrases de son livre sont équivalentes, comme sont équivalentes toutes les expériences de l'homme absurde; chacune se pose pour elle-même et rejette les autres dans le néant. . . .[5]

Sartre hesitated to call Camus's work a novel, for all that, precisely because its present was too flat, too complete to suggest an ongoing future, a "durée continué, la présence manifeste de l'irréversibilité du temps."[6] Camus's present resolved itself into a "succession de présents inertes" in Sartre's eyes, yet it is along this line of successive presents that the New Novel was to develop.

Thus eliminating the omniscient author or narrator removed any intermediary between the reader and the "subjectivités-points-de-vue"; the reader was made to enter directly into each consciousness, to coincide successively with each one. Joyce had captured a certain *réalisme brut* by just such direct transcription of the fictional subjectivity without mediation or distance. Problematically, however, direct transcription of a single subjectivity presumed direct transcription of the time of that single subjectivity, which was impossible to realize literally in a work of fiction. On the other hand, any manipulation of time in the novel would imply an intervention on the part of the author, which Sartre was seeking to avoid at all costs. Sartre was forced to conclude with his own version of the "fictitious" nature of every novel, which was not far different, in its initial assumptions, from the classical notion of the fictitious nature of any work of art. The only way of overcoming this temporal impasse was for the novelists to intervene and yet to mask his intervention insofar as he was able by resorting to purely esthetic techniques, by constructing a number of *trompe-l'oeil*, and by "lying" in order to tell the truth.

To make the temporality of each novel present, therefore, Sartre did not advocate exclusive use of the present tense. He always returned to the concept of artifice, or *trompe-l'oeil,* as necessary to simulate a continually evolving present moment.

In "Qu'est-ce que la Littérature?" he noted, "Ce n'est pas en changeant le temps du verbe mais en bouleversant les techniques de récit qu'on parviendra à rendre le lecteur contemporain de l'histoire."[7]

With an eye to making the story present to the reader, then, the temporal enigma posed by Sartre—to create one's characters consistently in a present sense even though consigned to a series of past events—precipitated the veritable outburst of fictional theories and experiments which have been preoccupying French critics and novelists for at least two decades. Consciously or unconsciously, each new writer seemed to react to Sartre's theory by discovering his own satisfactory fictional rendering of the series of present moments originally advocated by Sartre.

## Pouillon's codification

In 1946 Jean Pouillon codified Sartrean precepts into an inclusive theory of the novel published under the title *Temps et roman*.[8] He devoted a major portion of his book to a definition of the possible forms point of view assumed in the novel. His initial points paralleled those of Sartre. Each form signified a mode of comprehension chosen by the author through which the reader had access to the novel. The author's and reader's perspectives coincided vis-à-vis the novel, with the fictional character serving as their point of contact. The fictional character should evolve in a psychologically meaningful way during the course of the novel; that is, over a period which would constitute the character's private time, or *durée*.

Pouillon more clearly systematized the Sartrean dichotomy between the interior and the exterior perspectives of the fictional character. His categories were applicable to all novels, both past and present, and established two basic modes of comprehending the work of fiction. One was by considering the fictional character as a separate entity isolated from his surroundings, or fictional world, as represented in the classical approach to fiction. This vision *par derrière* was one in which the author, hence the reader, remained separate from the protagonist in order to see his gestures and to hear his words, but especially to consider objectively his psychic life. There was a direct vision of the psyche in this kind of novel, but it retained the duality of seen and seer; there was no identification between the author or the reader and the character. Balzac's creation of types was designated by Pouillon as the best example of this approach.

Pouillon's opposing mode of comprehension was one in which the fictional character was considered an inherent part, indeed the organizing force, of the world in which he existed, so that together the character and his fictional world formed a subject-world complex which had to be totally comprehended at once. The reader participated in the fictional world through the central character who, as narrator or translucid protagonist, remained ephemeral because he primarily served as a filter for the reader's *vision avec,* or participation in the fictional world. Neither the reader's nor the author's point of view was privileged; both took part in the fictional experience along with the protagonist.

Pouillon claimed with Sartre that the present was the privileged literary tense; the past was understood from the present, so that the present was the source of temporality rather than its residue. Both theorists contended that the tense of a verb did not express temporal relationships, but that it did express the relationship between what is narrated and the narrator or reader. Pouillon further suggested that the first person facilitated the use of the present tense. He thereby linked person to tense in a way which soon became one of the most disputed points among New Novelists and critics.

In short, French novelists inherited around 1950 quite literally the notion originally proposed by Sartre that organization of each fictional world depended upon the author's handling of point-of-view-subjectivities presented in a succession of present moments represented by each event in the development of the story. Technically, this reduced itself to a definite determination of person along with the manipulation of tense and other *trompe-l'oeil* in such a way as to create a series of seemingly present events.

## Subsequent novelists

The omniscient author had been successfully excised by Sartre, but subsequent novelists tended to tip the scale too far in the opposite direction by trying to place an omniscient reader at the narrational apex. Sartre had equally balanced the author's and reader's perspectives in such a way as to force the reader, in fact, to serve as ultimate interpreter. Novelists following Sartre felt obliged, therefore, to induce the reader to participate more actively in deciphering or in thoroughly "comprehending" the work of fiction. Their enticements had to be incorporated within the fabric of the novel itself.

That Sartre specifically left the final esthetic interpretation of the novel up to the reader explains in great part the multiplicity of significations which began to proliferate in each New Novel. Writing with an eye ever toward reader interpretation, the New Novelist both liberated his fictional world by making it more autonomous and complicated it by endowing it with a multiplicity of possible significations. Both writers and critics noted the newly felt presence of things burdened with the weight of their recently acquired importance as symbols or correlates of what the novelist was trying to convey.

These ambiguities and multiplicities intrinsic to the New Novel, however, did not constitute wholly gratuitous events or totally unconnected incidents as were found, for example, in surrealist sequences. The New Novelist did posit a coherent world which was there for the reader to decipher; it was up to the reader to determine to what lengths he was willing to go in order to do so. In this respect, New Novels took on a commonly acknowledged "puzzle" aspect, causing them frequently to be compared to the mystery or detective story. In some instances, critics even claimed that specific New Novels—such as Robbe-Grillet's *Dans le Labyrinthe,* for example—ultimately defied any totally coherent reconstruction by the reader. In short, the New Novel has most often been described in recent years by the adjective "labyrinthine." Whether the critic evokes the novelist's labyrinthine style, labyrinthine presentation, or plot or awareness, the concept of the labyrinth has come to signify the New Novel itself. It constitutes a kind of archetypal image shared by those authors and critics who discuss the New Novel in any context, whether it is favorable or unfavorable, and clearly denotes their response to the confusing, enigmatic nature of these novels.

## Manipulation of person: Sarraute, Robbe-Grillet, and Butor

A novel is an action transmitted through various subjectivities, according to Sartre. Initially, the New Novelists tended to emphasize the second half of this Sartrean equation by numerous discussions and experiments centered around the narrative pronoun most appropriate to contemporary fiction. The Proustian *je* and the Gidean narrator-protagonist were already complex and multifaceted; New Novelists and critics further complicated the narrative pronoun by initiating theories about different "modalities" of person,[9] emphasizing in the main the first-person pronoun as the most appropriate to ally with the present tense they had taken over from Sartre. Thus, their interpretation of Sartre's unfolding present became quite literally the use of the grammatical present tense, and their adoption of Sartre's precept about persona became a literal use of the grammatical first person.

Nathalie Sarraute's theoretical treatise entitled *L'Ère du soupçon* announced in 1950 the beginning of a new era in French prose fiction based precisely on the role of the first-person pronoun.[10] Ostensibly a revolt against Sartre and the politically committed or philosophically oriented novel, Mme Sarraute's view proclaimed that both the novelist and his reader distrusted the fictional character and through him each the other. The fictional character was merely presumed necessary as a viable path of communication between author and reader, and almost disappeared as an independent entity in the wake of their mutual distrust.

The modern hero had degenerated into a being without contours, indefinable, and invisible; he had become an anonymous first person primarily reflecting different attitudes of the author. Still, Mme Sarraute opted for the first-person novel as the one most legitimate for both contemporary reader and author. The first person at least had the *appearance* of having lived his experience, of exemplifying that authenticity which the reader expected. Since it was most important to Mme Sarraute to portray the coexistence of contradictory sentiments and to render the complexity of psychological life, the novelist, in all honesty, should speak exclusively of himself. Fictional "characters," in Mme Sarraute's novels, therefore, surpassed even the Sartrean point-of-view-subjectivities in becoming pure points-of-view projected from the novelist's own subjective concerns, with none of the Sartrean freedom to choose themselves.

On the other hand, Mme Sarraute was the first novelist after Sartre to enlist the reader's cooperation in interpreting the novel as the most significant development of modern fiction:

Tout est là, en effet: reprendre au lecteur son bien et l'attirer coûte que coûte sur le terrain de l'auteur. Pour y parvenir, le procédé qui consiste à désigner par un "je" le héros principal, constitue un moyen à la fois efficace et facile.[11]

To write a novel in the first person was the best way to plunge the reader into the interior of the fictional world as the author was already plunged into it. In order to effect such direct involvement, Mme Sarraute transcribed not simply the "I" of normal dialogue, or *conversation,* nor even the conscious "I" of conventional interior monologue, but also the semiconscious "I" found in *sous-conversation,* or subterranean nascent states of emotion normally kept tacit. In this way each subjectivity was tripled and at least two subjectivities were necessary to the work of fiction. Although Mme Sarraute's points of view all stemmed from the novelist's subjective concerns on the real plane, on the fictional plane they never had a single center, but continually demanded multiple centers, or several points of view.

That these points of view lost their human embodiment as physical entities and became disembodied "supports" expressing "commonplaces" in a frantic attempt to assuage their "terrible desire to establish contact" (in Mme Sarraute's own words) clearly reflected the Sartrean notion of "bad faith" carried to its dehumanized extreme.

Since Mme Sarraute's fictional technique consisted entirely of transcribing conversations and subconversations, the present tense was inherent within her method. The narrative present foundered between intercommunications among her various subjectivities and intracommunications within each one. Point of view burst asunder, multiplied, and almost disappeared in her works written from the many perspectives projected from the single "I" of the author.

Nathalie Sarraute, then, in spite of becoming the first novelist after Sartre to set down her theoretical concerns in a manifesto specifically countering the master, based her theory on certain Sartrean precepts. She hailed reader participation in interpreting the novel as the fundamental approach to contemporary fiction, and in order to effect a direct involvement on the part of the reader, she recommended plunging him *in medias res* through the use of the first person. Unlike Sartre, however, she held the first person to be the most authentic, felt the novelist should create all his characters from his own single subjective "I," which speaks exclusively of itself. In the name of authenticity, which for Mme Sarraute was complex and multiform, she split and multiplied the first-person pronoun upon which she based her entire theory. In effect, she merely reduced Sartre's person and present time to the grammatically literal.

Most New Novelists and critics agreed with Mme Sarraute that rather than adding a reflective dimension to the novel, the first person is often merely a fictive device unifying the work in which it is found and which, therefore, precludes any critical questioning by the reader. In every case, opting for the first person by these novelists and critics became a matter of automatically forcing the reader to participate in the fictional experience along with the author. Existentialist critics and theorists, such as Pouillon, also approved of this method of unifying the novel, but added a cautionary note about too close identification between the fictive "I" and the reader, since fictive first persons, prone to the ever-present existential bad faith, might easily dupe the reader to the very same extent that first person himself was duped. The problem of point of view reduced itself for such authors to discovering a fictional "I" which both revealed and objectified itself without eliminating its distance from the reader. Broaching the old Brechtian problem of "distanciation," then, novelists preoccupied with the various modalities of person introduced into the contemporary novel this primarily theatrical notion.

Writers and critics more closely allied to the New Novel, such as Roland Barthes, Bernard Pingaud, Michel Butor, and Alain Robbe-Grillet, constructed elaborate theories about the use of various pronouns in works of fiction: from primitive to elaborate forms, from simple to compound significances, from objective to subjective uses, until, in the sixties, the question of narrative viewpoint appeared to be "one of the most ambiguous and unresolved aspects of fictional structure."[12]

By then the majority of all French novels were written exclusively in the first person, stressing the fact that these young writers were intent on not dominating their works of fiction as the omniscient author so deplored by Sartre. Indeed, one critic was led to remark, "Nothing marks these novelists more than their determination not to be present in their work."[13] And, similarly, another observed that "only in the twentieth century do mutations of perspective or points of view become conscious."[14] Traditionally, narrative pronouns had exclusively determined perspective in the novel, but the contemporary trend was to compound their significance if not to eliminate them entirely in order to force the reader to adopt the narrator's—and therefore the author's—point of view.

With the advent of Robbe-Grillet's early literary criticism, point of view in the novel was equated to the fixed position of the camera in film-making. Robbe-Grillet's statements revealed more about his own art than about that of the film-makers, of course, and to equate a literary technique—point of view— with a concrete, physical camera, early typified his tendency toward restricting perspective primarily to the concrete and the visual.

One of his earliest articles presented point of view specifically as a descriptive technique.[15] To describe a room full of books, for example, the camera must portray only external evidence from its single angle of vision, though any one of several methods of shooting might be chosen.

Pour décrire notre pièce encombrée de livres, l'objectif choisira un angle de vue donnant une idée d'ensemble de l'envahissement; ou bien il balayera les murs pour venir fixer son regard en un point particulièrement chargé; ou encore il fera se succéder une série de vues fixes caractéristiques. . . .[16]

In his critical essays collected under the title *Pour un nouveau Roman,* Robbe-Grillet further elaborated the most important characteristic feature he believed that modern fiction shared with the cinema, which was its preoccupation with the present.

Le cinéma ne connaît qu'un seul mode grammatical: le présent de l'indicatif. Film et roman se rencontrent en tout cas, aujourd'hui, dans la construction d'instants, d'intervalles, et de successions qui n'ont plus rien à voir avec ceux des horloges ou du calendrier.[17]

Rather than portray any form of chronological time or duration, Robbe-Grillet found that contemporary novels portrayed "le plus souvent, des structures mentales privées de 'temps.' "[18] A film unfolded in a perpetual present which rendered impossible any memory of the past or any certain knowledge of the future; "C'est un monde sans passé qui se suffit à lui-même à chaque instant et qui s'efface au fur et à mesure."[19]

Exactly as the length of the film determines its actual time, the only important character in a film is the spectator who imagines the story in his own head. Similarly, in the modern novel, Robbe-Grillet found time split from its ability to flow continuously, or its temporality in the Sartrean sense. It would be difficult to find a more literal, and thus distorted, interpretation of Sartre's series of present moments. Robbe-Grillet's depleted present moment which does not flow but remains an end in itself here replaces Sartre's present moment replete with past and future potential. Sartre's temporal ribbon is cut to shreds. Robbe-Grillet, pushing to its limit Camus's "série de présents inertes," describes time as cut off or separated from its temporality.

Dans le récit moderne, on dirait que le temps se trouve coupé de sa temporalité. Il ne coule plus. Il n'accomplit plus rien. . . . Ici l'espace détruit le temps et le temps sabote l'espace. La description piétine, se contredit, tourne en rond. L'instant nie la continuité. Or, si la temporalité comble l'attente, l'instantanéité la deçoit; de même que la discontinuité spatiale déprend du piège de l'anecdote.[20]

On the other hand, Robbe-Grillet openly followed Sartre's lead by soliciting the reader's participation in actively "inventing" the novel along with the author in a combined creative endeavor. Again Robbe-Grillet carries Sartre's notion to an extreme, however, by conceiving of the reader not merely as interpreter but also as independent creator and architect of whatever worlds he constructs, both fictional and real.

L'auteur aujourd'hui proclame l'absolu besoin qu'il a du concours [du lecteur], un concours actif, conscient, *créateur*. Ce qu'il lui demande, . . . c'est de participer à une création, d'inventer à son tour l'oeuvre—et le monde—et d'apprendre ainsi à inventer sa propre vie.[21]

In soliciting active reader-creation of the world—whether fictional or real—Robbe-Grillet highly overestimates most readers' creative potential. This especially obtains with respect to the contemporary disenchanted reader as he is most aptly depicted by Mme Sarraute's portrait of suspicion.

What Robbe-Grillet discounts in particular, as do most New Novelists beginning at least with Nathalie Sarraute, is the Russian-conceived notion of the novelist's "break through to the other." Indeed, these novelists create no "other"—no Anna Karenina, no Emma Bovary, not even a Roquentin—in their endless absorption with modalities of the self.

Finally, Robbe-Grillet's works exemplify the total disintegration and almost complete disappearance of the first person from his fictional world. With Maurice Blanchot's discovery that the "hole" or the "absence" of an event or of a person served as the very key permitting one to see into Robbe-Grillet's novels, other critics began to point out the *creux* or the *je-néant* or the "narrative consciousness" or the "consciousness window" provided by Robbe-Grillet's narrators—all of which supposedly indicated their "pure anonymous presence." Subscribing to the thesis that the way perspective is manipulated in a novel reveals its particular orientation, Olga Bernal first equated the anonymous point of view in *Dans le Labyrinthe* with the labyrinth of its title: "Il y a donc expérience du 'labyrinthe' en ce qui concerne le point de vue narratif. Le 'je' narrateur devient un 'on' narrateur, une voix anonyme."[22]

Adding to the complexities surrounding fictional perspective, Michel Butor, precisely paraphrasing Sartre, claimed that author and reader depend equally upon the fictional character who reveals as much about them as about himself. Once this fact is understood, the third person of every narrative becomes a first-person narrator. But the narrator of a novel is no more a first person to Butor than to his fellow New Novelists; he is "très exactement le point de vue auquel l'auteur invite [le lecteur] à se placer pour apprécier, pour goûter telle suite d'événements, en profiter."[23] The introduction of a narrator immediately poses the temporal question of situating the moment of the narrative with respect to the moment of its narration. The story is usually remembered, according to Butor, except in the case of interior monologue, which results from narration simultaneous with the moment the narrative events take place.

As to the modalities of person in a novel, Butor proposed the following scheme: the third person represents the fictional world, the first person represents the author, and the second person represents the reader. But all three relate to each other so that personal pronouns are incessantly displaced: *vous* represents a composite of *tu* and *il, je* combines *je* and *il*, while *nous* represents a combination of all these pronouns. As for the person to whom these pronouns refer, Butor claimed it best to dissociate any notion of a physical individual from the pronoun, but to interpret it, rather, "comme une fonction se produisant à l'intérieur d'un milieu mental et social, dans un espace de dialogue."[24] Further, among these "narrateurs flottants," "personnages pronominaux," and "groupes de possibilités qu'il est désormais difficile d'appeler personnages," the reader himself has been integrated into the fictional world and reduced as was the former fictional character into an "acteur grammatical parmi d'autres."[25] One begins to wonder with Jean Ricardou whether an "ère du pronominal" in the 1970s might not indeed replace Nathalie Sarraute's "ère du soupçon" of the 1950s.

The kind of mystification practiced here by Butor and his colleagues serves to prove that the more one tries to understand such ultra-French theoretical complexities, the more one loses sight of the New Novel as fiction. It becomes an excuse for critical ingenuity, the critics losing sight of the general truism that theories or manifestos *preceding* the literary works they describe correlate very little if at all with the works in their final form. Literary history shows that theories of literary creation follow the act of creation rather than precede it.

In general, New Novelists primarily interpreted the first-person narrator as limited and ephemeral or evanescent, if he did not disappear entirely, becoming an atemporal, floating, nonintegrated anonymous point of view without any concrete subjectivity at the last. The narrator was reduced simply to a filter, a camera lens, or a *creux*—an absence in the center of the novel.

As Bruce Morrissette has cleverly mused, "Once upon a time . . ." is one of the oldest of narrative beginnings invented; it is not until the twentieth century that the reader asks, "Who says that?"[26] Who, indeed, but a fictional character anchored in his fictional world? But how and in what way, by what device or formula or technique Sartre omitted to specify, thereby permitting each subsequent author to construe his own labyrinth. Critical standards were needed to indicate how to situate the point-of-view-subjectivity in his fictional field. Traditionally, critics assumed that by saying "I," the author made his perspective immediately self-evident. After 1950, however, Nathalie Sarraute split and multiplied the first-person pronoun, and Pouillon noted that the "I" could be objective as well as subjective. Robbe-Grillet reduced the first-person pronoun to a camera lens whose function primarily was to describe as a "narrative look" or "consciousness window," if not a *creux* or a *je-néant;* while Butor developed the compound aspects of various pronouns presumably more consonant with the multifaceted modalities of the contemporary fictive function which had lost all the properties of a person.

New Novelists, in theory at least, seemed to disregard the necessity, if not the inevitability, of certain conventions. To do away, for example, with Flaubertian realism is not to write pure fiction, as if independent of all arbitrary controls over writer and reader. Like any other, fictional intelligence orders. At their minimal least, characters must be situated spatially and temporally within their fictional world and with respect to one another. Otherwise, the floating, atemporal, nonintegrated point of view disappears and the fictional world disintegrates along with it. "The character and the phenomenon situate each other; a phenomenon must occur in the perspective of a character himself physically situated in the fictional field."[27]

But, according to the Sartrean convention, both person and tense combine intimately to determine "le point de vue narratif." It was not only the first-person pronoun, therefore, which became dominant and developed more and more complex subtleties at the hands of the New Novelists, but also, and perhaps even more profoundly, fictional time.

## Manipulation of time

The concomitant heritage from Sartre, therefore, was the temporal dichotomy intrinsic to the text of any novel: the hiatus between the moment an event occurred and the moment of its narration.[28] This hiatus was resolved in New Novels not only by making them all interior monologues, but more importantly, by reducing occurrence of every single event to its literal *present moment of narration*. Thus, an event occurs in a New Novel as one is reading about its occurrence, and neither before nor after the momentary reading of the text. Sartre had indeed stressed a "série de présents" as necessary to bridge the gap between occurrence and narration, but Sartre's "présent" was full of potential: the past and the future were interpreted from the present moment and included in it. More often than not in similarly creating a "série de présents," New Novelists cause the past to be "put into question" or negated.[29] Adhering literally to the present tense of narration, New Novelists note down the past merely as a mosaic of precisely hand-picked, remembered events which might be appropriate to the present momentary experience, but, in fact, are undifferentiated from it. Similarly, the future loses out also and occurs unpredictably as dream or wish or reality; it becomes evanescent, inextricably mingled with both present and past events. In other words, past, present, and future remain undifferentiated by tense or syntax in New Novels; together, all three constitute the simultaneous "présent" which occurs as it is being narrated.

Events in New Novels are not chronologically presented, therefore, once and for all indicative of a culminating point in the fictional character's experience which might constitute what

Joyce and others after him have termed an "epiphany."[30] Indeed, the *prise de conscience* is no longer the goal of the protagonist in a New Novel. The New Novel emphasizes, rather, the event as it is remembered, repeated, reiterated, or distorted in different contexts of the present moment. It tells a story in the process of occurring which Wilbur Frohock has described as a "continuum."[31] It is, however, the *discontinuous* quality of events in the New Novel occurring in undifferentiated states of remembering, dreaming, projecting, or perceiving which blatantly confuses; this totally achronological presentation strikes the reader first and foremost, destroying any continuity. Indeed, one is forced to read and reread in order to crystallize all the disparate elements and discontinuous events into a comprehensive universe. True, the reader becomes of necessity, therefore, a researcher or interpreter if not partial creator of the New Novel, as many New Novelists had predicted. All of which strongly suggests that Sartre's original plea to "empoigner," or implicate, the reader has succeeded in imposing itself as an esthetic necessity on every novel. For some, it is the loss or lack of chronology clearly defined in the New Novel which is its most unsettling aspect, its greatest defect; for others, such a mixed chronology presents its greatest challenge. The New Novelists interpret the series of presents in a literal way, indiscriminately mingling past, present, and future occurrences, often relating them only in the present tense in such a way as to break the temporal ribbon Sartre considered essential to every novel.

The present tense is not the only element indicating the present, however, according to Sartre's original notion, although a great number of articles and at least one entire book have been written on precisely this subject.[32] The New Novelists resort to various technical devices which would constitute what Sartre termed *trompe-l'oeil* and whose main function is to cause the sequence of events to *seem* to occur in the present moment. At least they attempt to cause the narrated events to occur along with the reading of the story, *as if* they were a series of present occurrences. Ultimately updating the

Sartrean notion so succinctly phrased by Pouillon of "respecting in the past the present that it was," New Novelists attempt in a most literal way to "respect in the present the present that it is."

Emphasis on the present tends also toward the dramatic, the theatre. "The new novel is proposing that fiction should be all scene or representation."[33] This view of the novel primarily as scene or representation stems from the James-Lubbock tradition which emphasizes the novel as drama and from the Joyce-Frank tradition which defines the novel as spatial literature with poetic overtones.[34] The New Novelist becomes quite literally a poet or a *metteur en scène*. He focuses his attention on décor, objects, gestures, or motifs which serve as correlatives of the emotional or intellectual mood of his point-of-view-subjectivities. Perspective in these circumstances, especially when couched primarily in descriptive terms as are the majority of New Novels, too often allies itself with the cinematic lens or the camera eye of focusing, close-ups, distancing, pan shots, montage, and the like. Indeed, the sequential frames of fixed, still poses found on a length of film strip closely approximate the primarily spatial sequences found in New Novels. But such a sequence of décor, motifs, or scenes is one with a vengeance, and in order to bring it to life and to comprehend it in its totality, John Sturrock urges the contemporary reader to learn with the New Novelists to "say it with things," rather than to "say it with flowers."

Sartre's assumption of a fictional world that is autonomous has been converted by the New Novelists into a world in which all significance and substance or meaning is self-reflective. Therefore the plots of New Novels, if plots there are, become circular or spiral. One must ultimately and always return to the fictional world itself rather than to the real world or to the reader or the author in order to understand each novel. All New Novels, therefore, have developed an "art-for-art" aspect, or the reflective dimension foreseen by Sartre in his introduction to Nathalie Sarraute's *Portrait d'un inconnu:* "Nous vivons à une époque de réflexion et le roman est en train de réfléchir sur lui-même."[35] The fictional world becomes itself the subject of the novel and the creative act is the creation of a creation or the story of creating a story. "These novels must *never* be read as examples in naive realism or naturalism, but as studied dramatizations of the creative process itself."[36] Artifice thus revealed allies the New Novel with Russian formalist preoccupations and the baroque. All of which best lends itself to the approach of structuralist interpreters. The created *monde romanesque* of each New Novel preempts the traditional notion of *récit*, which still remained all-important for Sartre.

Plot, or *récit*, in the New Novel is reduced to the literal sequence of words on the page. Description usurps dialogue as sufficiently "suspensive" to constitute the narrative "plot" for the contemporary novelist, attuned as he is to the pervading phenomenological insistence upon description per se. Robbe-Grillet's singular description of a slightly marred slice of tomato and his infamous "coffee-pot upon the table," for instance, have been recently hailed as self-sufficient "scriptural plots."

La cafetière fictive se livre dans une ambiguïté parfaite . . . cette cafetière fictive, par la nécessaire successive distribution des attributs, possède en sa littéralité, en l'étrange temporalisation scripturale qui la compose, l'exacte structure d'un *récit*. . . . Elle est elle-même, déjà, le récit. . . . Ainsi l'ordre que choisit la description pour présenter les diverses parties d'un tout, suffit à établir une intrigue.[37]

The spatio-temporal field of the novel has thus been reduced precisely to the space it occupies on the page and to the time it requires in the reading. Most New Novelists, like Simon and Robbe-Grillet, exclusively "rely on the coincidence of the time-scale of the narration with the time-scale of what is narrated,"[38] thus reducing time in the novel to a perpetual present unprecedented in its literal application to the present moment and in the variety of philosophical and literary interpretations it has fostered. Such a perpetual present juxtaposes fictional events into a pattern rather than a plot, a literary *assemblage* recently likened to Claude Lévi-Strauss's notion of creating myths by a kind of "bricolage intellectuel."[39] Indeed, it might not seem improper some day to view most New Novels as mythmaking vehicles.

The new fictional temporality depends strictly upon each textual sequence of words which are geared to create multiple ambiguities. The New Novel announces a revel in ambiguity, a delight in reflection—with all it contains of repetition and eternal return—expressed through a superimposition of images and syncretism of forms allowing multiple open-ended interpretations. In this way the New Novel hopes to engage the creative play of our imaginations by presenting artifice as artifice, by engaging our reflective consciousness in the act of reflection itself and by choosing reflected forms to open out the possibilities of the play element in our consciousnesses as well as in our lives.

The French novel from Sartre to Robbe-Grillet, then, has evolved from simplicity and clarity to complexity and ambiguity; from a clear temporality of the *récit* to a spatial series of scenes; from prosaic and narrative to poetic and theatrical modes; from the socially committed to the esthetically challenging pose; and finally from the *être* to the *paraître*. "What is at stake at present is the authority of a liar in a society swarming with people accepted and even revered for telling the truth."[40]

In the three chapters that follow, three novels will be inspected with a view to uncovering their several perspectives. They were selected as being representative of the evolution of the New Novel from Sartre to the present. In each of the novels examined, perspective is handled in a different way. More than merely innovative for its epoch, each work is exemplary of its author and of its time. The technical handling of perspective, with regard to the relationship between person and tense, structurally determines the fictional world revealed which in turn reflects its author's philosophical orientation. Perspective first evolves from Sartre's multifaceted "il" in

*L'Enfance d'un chef* to Camus's equally multifaceted "je" in *L'Etranger* and finally to a split between the two, both of which serve to determine perspective in Robbe-Grillet's *Dans le Labyrinthe*. All three authors manipulate tense in such a way as to create the impression of the ever-unfolding present narrative originally suggested by Sartre.

# CHAPTER 2

*Chaque modalité du point de vue renvoie à une ontologie.*
—Bruce Morrissette

# "BAD FAITH" IN *L'ENFANCE D'UN CHEF*

*L'Enfance d'un chef* is a nearly perfect example of Sartre's existential bias in fictional perspective. Although it is a traditional narrative related in the third person and the past preterite, Sartre has managed to limit perspective almost exclusively to that of his protagonist Lucien Fleurier. Lucien is an open character: everything he perceives, thinks, or feels is transcribed and is, theoretically, nothing but what he perceives, thinks, or feels. Neither do perceptions and thoughts of any other fictional character intervene in Lucien's story, nor does the author betray his presence in his fictional universe by interposing his own judgments, explanations, or comments.

Through subtle narrative devices, however, Sartre so insinuates his ironical voice into the story that by the end of *L'Enfance d'un chef* the reader gathers the precise impression of the protagonist that Sartre means him to have. At the last, after a long *prise de conscience,* Lucien arrives at complete understanding and acceptance of himself, while the reader and author condemn him as an inauthentic "salaud" and an anti-Semite.[1] Into this perspective so exclusively limited to his fictional protagonist, Sartre has subtly managed to introduce a duplicity. Yet, at the same time, he remains true to his theoretical *données* concerning point-of-view-subjectivities and the succession of present moments.

## Manipulation of time

With respect to temporality in *L'Enfance d'un chef*, the story proceeds chronologically, yet Sartre can be said to manipulate this chronology insofar as it represents Lucien's personal memory of time. The chronology of Lucien's story is based on a series of figures or leitmotifs which constitute the various stages of the boy's *prise de conscience*. As Lucien passes from one stage of consciousness to another, and as his consciousness broadens, new figures are introduced in such a way as continually to indicate the present stage at which Lucien finds himself. In this way Sartre conveys the cumulative effect of experience in the boy's consciousness as well as his evolution from one present stage of consciousness to the next. Sartre's juxtaposition of these leitmotifs is responsible in part for the *trompe-l'oeil* effect in which Lucien's expanding awareness seems to take place in a moment always "present" to the protagonist and thus to the reader.

The main leitmotif is carried through a cluster of subordinate ones. The central theme of *mensonge* is introduced into Lucien's story in the following way, for example:

Et maman raconta: mais peut-être qu'elle mentait. Peut-être qu'elle était autrefois un petite garçon et qu'on lui avait mis des robes—comme à Lucien, l'autre soir—et qu'elle avait continué à en porter pour faire semblant d'être une fille. Il tâta gentiment . . . [P. 150][2]

Introduced by Sartre at the outset, this theme of *mensonge* is exploited throughout the story as intrinsic to Lucien's universe. Lucien plays roles eternally, usually those assigned him by others, expressing on one level his existential bad faith, and on another the theatrical nature of his character. The story is, in fact, a drama staged within Lucien's consciousness, between himself and himself, as well as the external drama staged between Lucien and others. His burgeoning consciousness is the central player, so that the rest of the story gives way continually to its expression. The limiting of plot to a gradual development of themes, or leitmotifs, which become constant figures, such as this central one, *mensonge*, somewhat justifies esthetically the continual liberties Sartre takes with direct and indirect discourse. These leitmotifs not only constitute stages in Lucien's growth, but indicate as well the metaphysical aspect of the physical events occurring at each stage. The unity of many passages depends upon just such an introduction and development of a single theme, like *mensonge* in this passage, so that the chronological development of the story will pass from theme to theme, from figure to figure, as ascertained by the boy's subjective consciousness.[3] Thus the plot unfolds within Lucien's personal *durée* rather than in any other temporal mode.

Along with the use of unfolding leitmotifs, Sartre further manipulates time in *L'Enfance d'un chef* by abridging years and events on the one hand, and by introducing appropriate flashbacks on the other. Together, these three techniques form the *trompe-l'oeil* he originally proposed as a means of making the past-tense narrative seem to occur in an ever-unfolding present.

As for abridging time so that Lucien will grow from a very young boy to an adult during the course of his story, Sartre most frequently wedges brief temporal statements of events which normally transpire over a long period of time into his lengthy descriptions of Lucien's various emotional stages. During each emotional stage, therefore, time passes imperceptibly with only the briefest acknowledgment, if it is acknowledged at all.

As an adolescent, for instance, Lucien passes through a somnolent stage during which he wakes up every morning "endormi," so difficult is it for him to concentrate his attention. During a long description of Lucien's traits characteristic of this period of ennui, Sartre inserts the single sentence, "Il eut trois fois de suite le prix d'excellence" (p. 167). In one short statement three years pass practically unobserved except for the fact that Lucien presumably remains in his somnolent state for the entire time. Since this story is narrated in the third person, such abridgments cannot be interpreted as deriving from Lucien himself narrating his own story as would automatically be true in a first-person narrative.

Very often in flashbacks, too, Sartre's hand may be observed. When allusion is made to anterior events, for example, the memories recalled cannot always be interpreted as entirely innocent spontaneous memories of Lucien. They seem to have been hand-picked for the occasion. In the following example, for instance, Sartre sets off Lucien's thought by the conventional "il pensa." As the narrative progresses, point of view, though spanning time and space, remains with Lucien. The event Lucien remembers, however, while disclosing the boy's memory, clearly emphasizes Sartre's theme of *mensonge*. Lucien's "directed spontaneity" here allies *mensonge* to the theatrical, to disguise, and to his continual quest for the amusing.

Il pensa: ça n'est pas pour de vrai. Il aimait bien quand ça n'était pas pour de vrai mais il s'était amusé davantage le jour du Mardi Gras: on l'avait costumé en Pierrot. . . . [P. 148]

These subtle external interventions by leitmotifs, by time abridgments, and by carefully chosen flashbacks, however, are integral to the very spatio-temporal framework of Sartre's story. They are minimal in number, in content, and in their unassuming placement in the longer descriptive passages which expose Lucien's *prise de conscience*. They are filtered as exclusively as possible through Lucien's consciousness.[4] It is primarily when they contradict Lucien's present preoccupations that they seem to break out of his perspective. And yet, though the contradiction is there, the center of orientation remains principally with Lucien rather than shifting entirely to Sartre. In this sense, such external interventions weigh scarcely more than the proverbial author's thumb which always slightly tips the scale, and *L'Enfance d'un chef* develops largely without overt evidence of the author's presence. On this point, Wayne Booth has quite accurately commented: ". . . Though the author can to some extent choose his disguises, he can never choose to disappear."[5]

## Manipulation of person

With respect to internal aspects of the narrative, Lucien's thoughts and emotions are transcribed in such a way as to create an ambiguous point of view, which has been described quite felicitously as "narrated monologue."[6] Lucien's first-person subjective "I" interrupts the objective narrative periodically, so that he intervenes in his own story, as it were, rather than the author or another fictional character intervening as is traditionally the case.[7] It is in the vacillations between third and first person that Sartre's handling of perspective becomes most subtle and most telling. The use of the third person facilitates Sartre's establishment of a second perspective in a way which can be contrasted to Camus's use of the first person in *L'Étranger*. Whereas Camus objectifies the normally personal and confessional "I," Sartre personalizes the usually objective narrative "he." By "personalize," I mean that Sartre allows his protagonist's first-person commentary to express itself sporadically throughout his narrative. Lucien's interior monologue periodically expresses his discovery, his awareness, or his interpretation of his surroundings so that the reader is constantly drawn from an external description into Lucien's awareness of himself. It is undoubtedly through this subjective orientation that Sartre tries to establish Lucien as the central point-of-view-subjectivity of his story as well as to "respect in the past the present that it was," in *L'Enfance d'un chef*.[8] The story begins and ends with direct statements by Lucien which further enhance this subjective orientation of his point of view.

The first sentence of *L'Enfance d'un chef*, which is enclosed in quotation marks but not immediately attributed to anyone, originally establishes Lucien's story within his perspective. "Je suis adorable dans mon petit costume d'ange" (p. 147). This *je* is identified as Lucien only three lines later, at which time Sartre indicates to the reader where Lucien acquired this idea of being adorable in his angel costume; it is not a self-evaluation, but one suggested to him by a certain

Mme Portier. Immediately the dialectical movement of Lucien's *prise de conscience* is revealed; it is always from the exterior to the interior. From external events, whether comments or gestures, Lucien always derives his internal conclusion; there is no intuitive discovery in Lucien which does not derive from an external event. At the moment of interior discovery, both emotional and intellectual, Lucien's personal *je* often intervenes to express that revelation. In this way Lucien's self-discovery serves as the subject matter of the story, perspective is firmly anchored within his subjectivity-point-of-view, and this manner of presenting his awareness as growing out of surrounding events, as a series of discoveries culminating from disparate and often painful episodes, exhibits the primary function of what has been termed "contingency" in Sartre's work. Lucien's character is continually molded by exterior events, and is never fully formed until the last episode of self-realization during which he makes his final and definitive discovery: "C'est moi la cathédrale" (p. 239). This last discovery not only results from, but also replaces, all preceding events in Lucien's final choice of his own identity.

Lucien's apotheosis, however, is presented ironically. After his glorious vision Lucien expresses his discovery in a ludicrous, dramatic gesture which summarizes his character and is ascribed, again, directly to him in the last sentence of the story: " 'Je vais laisser pousser ma moustache,' décidat-il" (p. 241).[9] Thus, from the first direct expression of the child who discovers himself "adorable" in his "little angel costume," a sentiment to be forgiven perhaps in a very young child, to the last direct expression of the man who will "allow his mustache to grow" as evidence of his maturity which by now has become monstrosity, Lucien cuts a clownish figure through the naïveté and vanity of the expressions of his self-appraisal. The indulgent smile granted the young angel who enters hardens into contempt for the mustached man who exits, just as Lucien's character hardens into a solid "cathedral" from the ambiguous uncertainty of the "angel."

By weaving irony into the tapestry of Lucien's growth to maturity, Sartre creates a second perspective, antipathetic to the boy, which eventually wins out over the sympathetic exposition of the boy's struggle in growth. At the last the boy is in sympathy with himself; the reader and the author are not.[10]

In order to delineate more precisely the manner in which Sartre expresses this double point of view, I shall first examine more closely his juxtaposition of first and third persons which seem to interrupt each other continuously as the narrative progresses.

The first time Lucien erupts into his own story and assumes his own narrative occurs within the opening paragraph of the story:

Tout le monde lui dirait: ma jolie petite chérie; *peut-être que ça y est déjà, que je suis une petite fille;* il se sentait si doux en dedans. . . . [P. 147; italics mine]

Beginning with "peut-être que" Lucien's first person breaks through the objective narration into interior monologue. Although set off by semicolons, this interruption is not attributed directly to the child by quotation marks or by any other indication; in spite of its brevity, it produces the desired esthetic effect. During this opening description of confusion in the child between masculine and feminine identity, Lucien, for one brief second, intervenes in his own story at the point at which his internal comprehension crystallizes from what transpires around him. In spite of the brevity of this eruption into his own story, or because of it, Lucien's interior monologue serves as a climactic point of discovery within the boy's consciousness. Technically, his conscious expression breaks through the narrative form which then, almost immediately, takes over again. Yet all this is without warning; the shift is unprepared for grammatically.[11] In other words, Lucien's conscious expression is concomitant with his conscious discovery. He now expresses openly what has been happening around and within him in a confused or unconscious way. And the movement is always from the exterior to the interior, so that

Lucien is forever determined by others, by the words or the
actions of others around him, or by the events which happen
to him.

A second example of Lucien's first person capturing the
thread of his own story, interrupting the narrative and at the
same time casting doubt, creating a hiatus between himself and
his life, occurs shortly thereafter at the point where Sartre first
introduces the leitmotif of *mensonage* and which again begins
with "mais peut-être que. . . ."

Et maman raconta: *mais peut-être qu'elle mentait. Peut-être
qu'elle était autrefois un petit garçon et qu'on lui avait mis des
robes—comme à Lucien, l'autre soir—et qu'elle avait continué
à en porter pour faire semblant d'être une fille.* Il tâta gentiment. . . .

[P. 150; italics mine] [12]

A slight variation on this same technique of allowing
Lucien's perspective to break through the external narrative is
Sartre's frequent use of the neutral "ce" or "ça" to indicate
Lucien's subjective thought in place of the first person singular
"je." Rather than interrupt his narrative flow with the insertion
of the first person, Sartre frequently imposes Lucien's personal
perspective by using the impersonal "ce" or "ça" to summarize
a complex of preceding thoughts or events. The clause containing "ce" or "ca" occurs at precisely the same moment of
Lucien's realization as do those clauses attributed to his first
person. These expressions always indicate Lucien's point of
view as it inserts itself into the narrative stream. In the example already cited, for instance, which describes Lucien's
memory of the Mardi Gras, the neutral "ça" appears twice as
part of his interior monologue:

Il pensa: *ça n'est pas pour de vrai. Il aimait bien quand ça n'était
pas pour de vrai mais il s'était amusé davantage le jour du
Mardi Gras.* . . .

[P. 148; italics mine]

In the following description of his mother's friends,
Lucien's internal sensibility suddenly interrupts the external

description and interprets it in such a way as to impress it forever into his subjective consciousness:

Quand elles sont ensemble, elles mangent de tout et elles parlent et leurs rires mêmes sont graves, *c'est beau comme à la messe.*

[P. 153; italics mine]

This neutral voice not only expresses Lucien's interior thought, but also undercuts, interrupts, and stops the solemnity, or tragedy, or cruelty, inherent within a situation, so that Lucien never quite attains consciousness in this respect. Thus, by consigning Lucien's subjective awareness to the neutral "ce," Sartre very often interrupts or stops the dramatic élan which has been gathering momentum for some time exactly as Brecht would do with his *Verfremdungseffekt,* translated variously as "distanciation" or "alienation effect." The neutral *ce* in these instances is contained within a terse clause which follows long periodic sentences. The brevity of these clauses emphasizes their import. They summarily express Lucien's internal evaluation of preceding external events in such a naïve way that criticism is implicit within their expression.

The following passage, for example, relates the dream Lucien has the night he spends in his parents' bedroom, and precipitates his decision never again to do so:

Le lendemain Lucien était sûr d'avoir oublié quelque chose. Il se rappelait très bien le rêve qu'il avait fait: *papa et maman portaient des robes d'anges, Lucien était assis tout nu sur son pot, il jouait du tambour, papa et maman voletaient autour de lui; c'était un cauchemar.* Mais, avant le rêve, il y avait eu quelque chose. . . .

[P. 149; italics mine]

This paragraph, too long to quote in its entirety, is characteristic of Sartre's handling of perspective. It is as if Sartre deliberately blurs his focus first one way, then the other, in describing Lucien's vain effort to recapture what he has forgotten. Reminiscent of Henry James's technique in manipulating his young heroine's point of view in *What Maisie Knew,* the device reveals enough in this instance for the forgotten event to dawn upon the reader, although it remains obscure to the boy. After Sartre's initial objective description of Lucien's having forgotten something followed by the boy's dream of the preceding night told from his point of view as indicated above, Lucien's perspective regresses further in time to some half-forgotten event which preceded his dream, then abruptly returns to Lucien's present experience which, still colored by the preceding night, is interrupted once again by the imposition of his point of view and leads, finally, to his decision never again to sleep in his parents' room.

Although Lucien's point of view seems to halt the unfolding narrative, or to bring it up short, necessitating a change of direction thereafter, it also conveys the impression of clearer focus than the objective narrative preceding and following it. It asserts itself sporadically, when Lucien grasps and sums up his situation. Since Lucien's grasp falls short of its mark, the focus is never truly sharp, the picture never quite clear to him, although the following passage would seem to materialize the forgotten moment in a concrete vision.

Tout à coup il crut que ça y était; *s'il y pensait encore un tout petit peu, il allait retrouver ce qu'il cherchait. Le tunnel s'éclaira d'un pâle jour gris et on voyait remuer quelque chose.* Lucien eut peur et poussa un cri: le tunnel disparut.

[P. 149; italics mine]

Again Lucien's point of view captures the narrative, and offers in this instance a good example of objective correlative in Sartre's work.[13] The concrete image of the tunnel represents the target of the boy's quest; yet rather than allow it to materialize completely or follow it to its ultimate conclusion, Lucien becomes frightened of it and dissociates himself from it. This will prove to be Lucien's constant experience in life, and Sartre's irony becomes ever more mordant as Lucien's perspective broadens.[14]

Finally, the neutral "ce" indicates Lucien's most intimate discoveries, most personal evaluations, in terms in which the irony is self-evident. While undergoing a stage of Cartesian doubt, for instance, Lucien has his perplexity formulated in the following words which, though not attributed directly to him, could only come from his perspective: "La perplexité ne passait toujours pas: *c'était comme une envie d'éternuer*" (p. 173). Or shortly thereafter, when crossing the path of the son of his father's foreman, Lucien dramatizes: *"C'était l'occasion de se prouver qu'il était un chef"* (p. 173). This opportunity fails, compounding Lucien's doubts about the reality of his existence.

In context, Lucien's evaluations usually provoke ironic humor. After an initial exposure to Freud's work on dreams, Lucien apostrophizes:

*Ce fut une révélation.* "C'est donc ça, se répétait Lucien en marchant au hasard par les rues, c'est donc ça! . . . Parbleu, pensa-t-il, j'ai un complexe."

[P. 178; italics mine]

Less humorous is Lucien's eventual cruelty and anti-Semitism, where the neutral "ce" retains its ironical, satirical edge, but loses its humor. During the description of Lucien's and his friends' bloody physical attack on the little old Jew in the street, the following sentence is wedged in among others objectively describing the skirmish: *"C'était très amusant"* (p. 227). Although Lucien's constant quest for amusement is readily visible here, this neutral sentence might extend in this instance to the entire gang of adolescents. Similar to the many other phrases beginning with "ce," however, this statement is best attributed to Lucien. Sartre retains Lucien's personal expression even in instances which might ambiguously refer to the general, anonymous "on." In this way, events are constantly referred to Lucien's perspective, which continues to serve as the source of their occurrence.

Later, when Lucien is caught in his own anti-Semitic game and refuses to shake hands with the young Weill at a social gathering, humor and even satire seem to have disappeared from his expression: "Il haussa nerveusement les épaules: *c'était un désastre*" (p. 234; italics mine). Although

Lucien will soon learn to salvage this disaster, acknowledging it instead as intrinsic to his "moral health" and "commitment," he seems here to recognize its immoral implications. In this instance, the neutral "ce" evidently applies to the disgrace of his social comportment, and thus to the external event as is usually the case, but it also applies to his ideological failure as an anti-Semite. For the first time, Lucien's point of view expresses exactly his internal as well as external state, eliminating, therefore, Sartre's usual humorous or ironic contradictions.

In the following description of Lucien's family moving to Paris, the last phrase beginning with "ce" relates this spatial transition to Lucien immediately and directly: "Quand les Fleurier s'installèrent à Paris, *ce fut un éclair de magnésium*" (p. 168; italics mine). The flash can only refer to Lucien's experience of the move, and not to that of his parents. The entire move is reduced to this short sentence in which the event itself, which would chronologically be of long duration, is subordinated to Lucien's experience of it.

Sartre very often presents factual events in this manner. The event is announced in the most cryptic phrase possible, so that it appears to be gratuitous until it is later developed and related more solidly to Lucien's experience. Sometimes these events do not attract Lucien's conscious attention; they are mentioned briefly as they occur, but stay out of the range of Lucien's focus. In this way, Sartre constructs a kind of criticism of his protagonist by factual contradiction. Many events unacknowledged by Lucien contradict his struggle with his self-awareness and thus create irony. As a child, Lucien undergoes a siege of scarlet fever, for instance, which appears to be an utterly gratuitous event unrelated to any specific point of view:

Le lendemain ils parlèrent du père Noël et Lucien fit semblant de les croire: il pensait que c'était dans leur rôle; ils avaient dû voler les jouets. *Au mois de février, il eut la scarlatine et s'amusa beaucoup.*
Quand il fut guéri, il prit l'habitude de jouer à l'orphelin.

[P. 151; italics mine]

The sentence beginning "Au mois de février" indeed seems to convey a gratuitous event, except for the verb "s'amusa," which is at once consonant with the dominant theme of pretense or "faire semblant" in this passage and an ironic comment on Lucien's experience of illness. His quest for amusement seems to foreshadow the long subsequent passage in which he plays at being an orphan. The insignificance of his real illness contrasted with the richness of his imagined play is to be noted. Whatever transpires in Lucien's imagination, including past events recalled, dreams, or reveries of the future, it is the imagined events which always predominate over real events.[15]

Certain real events explicitly contradict Lucien's dreams, revealing in some instances the double life he leads, or "bad faith," exemplified by the discrepancy between his belief and his conduct. After a long internal struggle with the concept of God which finally reduces itself to a ritual by which Lucien attempts to exonerate himself, he finally renounces the whole "game" in the following terms:

Mais Lucien se lassa de ce jeu parce qu'il fallait faire de trop gros efforts et puis finalement *on ne savait jamais si le bon Dieu avait gagné ou perdu.* Lucien ne s'occupa plus de Dieu. Quand il fit sa première communion, M. le curé dit que *c'était le petit garçon le plus sage et le plus pieux de tout le catéchisme.*
[P. 159; italics mine]

Sartre's double-edged satire of the priest's blindness here, as well as of Lucien's bad faith, occurs, not through any sort of direct intervention on the part of the author, but, true to his theory, through the words of another subjectivity anchored in Lucien's fictional world.

Another such short passage which contrasts Lucien's external behavior with his internal preoccupations is the one previously cited describing Lucien's long period of somnolent inattention to his studies. Inserted into the description of this rather long period of Lucien's ennui during which he does not make the slightest effort at his studies, appears the single

statement: "Il eut trois fois de suite le prix d'excellence"
(p. 167).

An ironical second perspective results from the contrast of
such external facts of which Lucien is aware, but to which he is
inattentive, with his internal preoccupations. The esthetic
effect of such passages is to enhance the hiatus between much
of the boy's external life and his interpretation of these same
events. Although not developed at any great length, Sartre's
second perspective is always suggested by brief ironical
touches such as these factual statements which run counter to
the mainstream of Lucien's growth. Although the gap widens
as Lucien matures, the reader is consistently aware of a separation between Lucien's experience and his interpretation of that
experience. Parallel to the external-internal hiatus, Sartre also
develops an internal *dédoublement* within Lucien himself, so
that the boy is never at one with himself or with his universe.
In this respect Lucien concretely embodies Sartre's philosophical concept of bad faith, and inauthenticity.

Along with the frequent use of *ce* and the external descriptive fact, and similar in their descriptive tone and neutral-
izing effect, belong the less frequent phrases of "il y a" or "il
se trouve" and "on." "On" replaces "je" very often, permitting
Sartre to introduce Lucien's point of view into an objective,
descriptive sentence, with but one difference. Whereas the
first person "je" is reserved for climactic moments of self-
discovery within Lucien's consciousness, "on" merely prolongs
description in a more neutral tone, although it also indicates a
shift in perspective to Lucien. The following example will
suffice to demonstrate Sartre's use of "on" in place of Lucien's
first person.

Il boudait souvent: c'était aussi un jeu mais plutôt amusant. *On
faisait de la peine à maman, on se sentait tout triste et rancuneux,
on devenait un peu sourd avec la bouche cousue et les yeux
brumeux, au dedans il faisait tiède et douillet comme quand on
seul au monde.* Lucien ne pouvait plus sortir de ses bouderies. . . .
*est sous les draps le soir et qu'on sent sa propre odeur; on était*
[P. 157; italics mine]

Comparable to the use of "ce" and "on," Sartre's use of "il y a" often relates to Lucien's point of view but does not always emanate directly from him. " 'Qu'est-ce que je suis, moi?' *Il y avait cette* brume, enroulée sur elle-même, indéfinie. 'Moi!' Il regarda au loin . . ." (p. 171; italics mine). Here the expression "il y a" continues the description of Lucien's internal awareness before the external descriptive narrative takes over again.

## Irony: Lucien's naïveté

Brief mention may be made of Sartre's frequent use of irony based upon the naïveté of Lucien. As with Voltaire's *Candide,* the young boy's thoughts, remarks, and interpretations of events are presented as so naïve that the reader is struck by the discrepancy between events as they are related and the boy's grasp of these events. Technically, exaggeration prevails here. Such exaggerated naïveté not only disengages the reader from any sympathy with Lucien, but also sharply criticizes the boy. The naïveté of any child or adolescent need not imply negative criticism, but Lucien's sensitivity to the ugly rather than to the beautiful, his resorting to cruelty rather than to kindness, and the inane metaphors of his smugness condemn him by his own expression in the eyes of the reader. Humor often prevails, but it is ironic humor, again, in which the irony eventually tips the scale away from whatever humor is initially suggested, so that the pause which might occasion at first only a wry smile resolves itself more and more frequently, as the boy matures, into moral condemnation on the part of the reader.

As a very young child Lucien discovers the solidity or impenetrability of things as compared with his own fragility. He flatters and insults by turns the chestnut tree, for example, in his back yard.

Mais l'arbre resta tranquille, tranquille—comme s'il était en bois. Le soir, à diner, Lucien dit à maman: "Tu sais, maman, les arbres, eh bien, ils sont en bois" en faisant une petite mine étonnée que maman aimait bien.                                          [P. 155]

Rather than simply ironic humor, however, Lucien's comment introduces his eternal search for a solid foundation applicable to himself so that he will be forever defined. Ironic as well, but without humorous relief, is Lucien's first experience of incomprehensible rage. In the effort to sort out whether he loves his mother or God most, Lucien runs into the garden, where the following scene takes place:

Il regarda le gros buisson d'orties avec défiance; on voyait bien que c'était un endroit défendu; le mur était noirâtre, les orties étaient de méchantes plantes nuisibles, un chien avait fait sa commission juste aux pieds des orties; ça sentait la plante, la crotte de chien et le vin chaud. Lucien fouetta les orties de sa canne en criant: "J'aime ma maman, j'aime ma maman. . . ." Il répéta: "J'aime ma maman" mais sa voix lui parut étrange, il eut une peur épouvantable et s'enfuit d'une traite jusqu'au salon. De ce jour Lucien comprit qu'il n'aimait pas sa maman.     [P. 154]

After presenting Lucien's discovery in direct discourse, Sartre seems to detach himself from the scene in order to make a conclusive, analytic remark. Though Lucien's own thoughts are predominant here, the final statement is in such contrast to the preceding action that Sartre's intrusion is unmistakable.

Later, throughout Lucien's adolescent crises, Sartre's ironic humor continually reveals itself through the naïveté of the boy's own expression. While preoccupied with suicide, Lucien voices the following fatuous paradox: "Je me tue parce que je n'existe pas. Et vous aussi mes frères, vous êtes néant" (p. 174). Or, again, during this same period: "Il était trop sensible pour faire un chef mais non pour faire un martyr" (p. 174).

After reading Freud on dreams, Lucien exclaims silently, "Parbleu, . . . j'ai un complexe" (p. 178). This statement carries the force of "Eureka!" or "I've found it at last" for the boy. Shortly thereafter, however, Lucien decides, naïvely again: "C'était bien joli d'avoir des complexes mais il fallait savoir les liquider à temps" (p. 181).

Sartre's humor most often mocks Lucien's attempts at
finding solidity, a permanent foundation or final definition of
his own personality. Whatever represents stasis, immutability.
solidity, or inability to change is fair game for Sartre's ironic
wit. It is Lucien who ought to suffer in his continual quest for
whatever solid identity might resolve his human condition, but
on the whole he does not suffer because of his very naïve comprehension of what takes place around and within him.

With regard to Lucien's experience with Bergère, Sartre
increases his irony. Lucien never comprehends the experience
being prepared for him, even when his own emotions reveal the
danger.

Lucien sortait de ces entretiens la tête en feu, il pensait que
Bergère était un génie, mais il lui arrivait de se réveiller la nuit,
trempé de sueur, la tête remplie de visions monstrueuses et
obscènes et *il se demandait si Bergère exerçait sur lui une bonne
influence.*

[P. 189; italics mine]

The last phrase beginning "il se demandait" contrasts
critically by its naïve expression with the preceding experience.
Sartre's attempt to stay exclusively within Lucien's point of
view facilitates this kind of irony.

Under Bergère's influence, Lucien sees himself as
Rimbaud, and expresses in an inane metaphor, "Il commençait
à croire qu'il aurait la vie brève et tragique d'une fleur trop
belle" (p. 190). The frequency of Lucien's naïve evaluations
of Bergère, such as "Lucien pensait qu'il était bien agréable
d'avoir un grand frère si indulgent et si compréhensif" (p.
193), and "Il trouvait admirable que Bergère fut à la fois si
profond et si gamin" (p. 194), effectively builds dramatic
tension for the final scene between the two. Such evaluations
are dangerous for the reader who, especially upon a first
reading, is tempted to sympathize or to identify with Lucien.
Sartre purposely leaves such events open to question; it is not
until subsequent events prove the corrupting influence of
Bergère's friendship that the reader fully realizes in retrospect Sartre's ironic intent.

Lucien's further experience with Berthe, the young working girl, reinforces the irony toward his attitudes at this stage, but with little comic relief. Attempting to seduce Berthe, Lucien considers her a "born victim," and his "thing." Although he does not consummate his attempted seduction, Lucien washes his hands with perfumed soap before drinking his tea, with the thought that he is no longer a virgin. This same ironic aspect of Lucien's expression continues to develop with more and more exaggeration and with less and less comic relief until the final pomposity of his, "Seulement, ce coup-ci, c'est moi la cathédrale!" (p. 239).

Finally, what is the result of these various techniques used by Sartre in his attempt to remain closely confined to Lucien's point of view? Sartre, as has been suggested throughout this inquiry into the perspective of *L'Enfance d'un chef,* makes himself both an accomplice and a traitor with respect to Lucien. He establishes a definite duplicity on his part; without intervening in a flagrant manner, he succeeds in satirizing his protagonist and in inciting the reader to do likewise. This is a subtle tactic in the sense that certain readers are tempted to identify with Lucien.[16] Sartre encourages this temptation by apparently adopting Lucien's point of view, but in the end he sabotages his protagonist. The tactic of an author sabotaging his protagonist whose point of view he pretends to adopt is traditional, well established since Voltaire's time, at least. In *L'Enfance d'un chef* Sartre develops it, perhaps, to perfection.

In order to expose Lucien's bad faith, Sartre's attitude toward him becomes necessarily one of bad faith. This conclusion tends to corroborate Sartre's theoretical supposition that to determine how perspective is handled in any given work of fiction is to gain insight into that author's philosophical orientation.

Yet, it is not the other fictional subjectivities who condemn Lucien's bad faith in *L'Enfance d'un chef;* rather, it is the author and the reader who do so. The reader participates in the fictional world by snapping up all the bait of the author, by retaining all of Sartre's subtle interventions which ultimately condemn Lucien.[17] Sartre promotes a complicity between the reader and the author in *L'Enfance d'un chef*, who eventually turn out to be antipathetic to the fictional protagonist. In *L'Étranger,* likewise, Camus will establish a complicity between author and reader, but, contrary to Sartre's antipathy, Camus will cause the reader to become ever more sympathetic to his fictional protagonist during the course of his story. Where Sartre speaks in the ironic mode, Camus will speak in the lyric.

# CHAPTER 3

*L'art, ce mentir vrai, c'est la façon de plaider pour ce monde,
si nous voulons y vivre.* —Louis Aragon

*Ainsi, le censeur crie ce qu'il proscrit. L'ordre du monde aussi
est ambigu.* —Albert Camus

*Nous ne nous étonnerons pas que, roman de l'ambiguité,*
L'Étranger *soit un roman ambigu.* —J.-C. Pariente

# AMBIGUITIES IN *L'ÉTRANGER*

Camus takes one step further toward unifying fictional perspective and ridding the novel of its omniscient author in the Sartrean sense by writing *L'Étranger* in the first person, although it remains predominantly in the past tense. In this work, however, Camus's first person is no less ambiguous than his past tense, so that ambiguities found in both point clearly toward perspective as it is applied in the New Novel. In other words, Camus's "objective" first person and his "present" past tense foreshadow not only the literal confining of perspective to some form of interior monologue, but also the blatant creation and cultivation of the ambiguous perspective adopted by the majority of French novelists after 1950.

Traditionally, the single protagonist relating various events of his life in the first person naturally unified point of view within his single perspective, theoretically eliminating even those subtle interventions such as were permitted Sartre by narrating Lucien's story in the third person. Since Camus's first person, however, has been taxed by every critic since A. Nicolas's thesis of 1955 with representing a third person, and since, contrary to literary tradition, his first person precludes introspection, Camus makes it possible to introduce "narrated monologue" into a story told literally as an interior monologue. Thus, he profits from the various possibilities of surreptitiously insinuating his own opinion and expression "in and above and beyond" Meursault's words in the subtle Joycean way, as, for example, in the instances of Meursault's profundity and tendency to moralize at the last.

But before discussing the ambiguities fostered by Camus's use of narrated monologue, let us first discover those ambiguities which stem from Camus's adroit manipulation of time.

## Manipulation of time

Although point of view in *L'Étranger* is solidly centered within the single protagonist, Meursault, it focuses alternately upon his *moi présent,* or his narrating presence, and upon his *moi passé,* or his remembered participation in the past. This continual vacillation of a single point of view between two separate moments results in temporal confusion. The events narrated have evidently preceded their narration, but the moment of their narration is obscured. When is the present moment at which the narrator speaks in relation to the past events about which he is speaking? This relationship constitutes the crux of the perspective problem raised by every novel written in the first person.

Camus manages by adroit manipulation of these two temporal moments to give the impression that events occur as the story progresses, whereas, in actuality, the events recounted have taken place in the past and are narrated as remembered exclusively by Meursault. The narrative tension thus created becomes acutely dramatic in the final chapter when Meursault focuses upon his condemnation and the possibility of escaping it: upon the meeting of past and present for a possible future or upon the reconciliation of past events with present realities which deny him any future whatsoever.

The several ways in which Camus establishes this illusion of an unfolding present are not easily discernible upon an initial reading of *L'Étranger*. Primarily, Camus's great innovation is to choose a conversational past tense, the *passé composé*, rather than the traditional literary *passé simple*. In addition, he adds numerous temporal indicators of the present, or "false presents," to the few true indications of the present, which make a final impact of the complete moment sufficient unto itself.[1] In this respect, Camus clearly exploits Sartre's notion of *trompe-l'oeil* with regard to time in the novel, even though he originally did so a number of years before Sartre's entire theory appeared in print. As yet unaware of the Sartrean precepts in their entirety, Camus succeeded brilliantly *avant la lettre* in respecting Sartre's existential bias in his novel. Contrary to Sartre's intent to simplify, however, perspective in *L'Étranger* is infinitely more complex and ambiguous than in *L'Enfance d'un chef,* and it seems clear today that Camus willfully rendered it so. Again in this respect, as well as in others, Camus's work serves as a clear transition between Sartre and the New Novel.

### Sartre's appraisal of *L'Étranger*

Sartre commented at length upon the present impression afforded by Camus's choice of the *passé composé* rather than the *passé simple* in *L'Étranger*. He maintained that the "reality" of a sentence such as "Il se promena longtemps" consists principally of verbal action, with its transitive quality intact, which supposes a future. By contrast, "Il s'est promené longtemps" hides the "verbality" of the verb, weakening its transitive quality to a past participle accompanied by the passive auxiliary "être," so that the reality of the sentence becomes the noun without projection or link between past and future.[2] Not only is the independence of the isolated moment thus emphasized, but also its present quality dominates its past. Meursault's *moi passé* is not so far removed from his *moi présent,* according to Sartre, as would be true if Camus had used the *passé simple* in *L'Étranger*.

In developing his thesis that "each sentence is a present" in *L'Étranger*, Sartre makes a syntactical analysis of Camus's style in order to prove that each sentence constitutes an isolated independent temporal unity without causal links or ties to any other sentence. Sentences follow each other in a disjunctive or additive fashion, or in opposition to one another as stylistic exemplification of the "absurd" experience. "Toutes les phrases de son livre sont équivalentes, comme sont équivalentes toutes les expériences de l'homme absurde,"[3] claimed Sartre, equating every present moment to every other present moment.

In spite of Sartre's accuracy in his stylistic analysis of *L'Étranger*, especially with regard to this disjunctive quality of Camus's sentences and their origin in the American "behaviorist" novel, it was not until twenty years later that Brian T. Fitch strongly protested against Sartre's separation of Camus's style from Meursault's narrating presence: "Sartre en a tout de même manqué l'essentiel en isolant le style de ce qui est . . . sa raison d'être: le personnage du narrateur."[4] Rather than fundamental to the personality of Meursault, M. Fitch believes that this "absurd" alienation was only an impression due to the lapse of time between the events narrated and the narration of them.[5] More recently linguists, such as J.-C. Pariente and André Abbou, interpret Meursault's absurdity in terms of a personal language crisis which actively highlights, through such disjunctive figures, 1) the usual ambiguities in the spoken word, 2) man's ineptitude and helplessness to master language, and 3) the impostures which normally hide behind words.[6]

Also belying Sartre's judgment that, in Camus, all present moments are equated is the clear experiential difference for Meursault of moments that are portrayed in terse, lucid, and primarily verbal prose, and those portrayed in lyrical, emotional, poetic prose characterized primarily by nouns and adjectives. The following passage, for example, is primarily verbal and attentive to each chronological moment:[7]

Comme j'aime beaucoup le café au lait, j'ai accepté et il est revenu un moment après avec un plateau. J'ai bu. J'ai eu alors envie de fumer. Mais j'ai hésité parce que je ne savais pas si je pouvais le faire devant maman. J'ai réfléchi, cela n'avait aucune importance. J'ai offert une cigarette au concierge et nous avons fumé.

[P. 1129]

By contrast, the next passage consists predominantly of nouns and adjectives and, although still chronological, the moments are widely separated in time and in space:

Il y a eu encore l'église et les villageois sur les trottoirs, les géraniums rouges sur les tombes du cimetière, l'évanouissement de Pérez (on eût dit un pantin disloqué), la terre couleur de sang qui roulait sur la bière de maman, la chair blanche des racines qui s'y mêlaient, encore du monde, des voix, le village, l'attente devant un café, l'incessant ronflement du moteur, et ma joie quand l'autobus est entré dans le nid de lumières d'Alger et que j'ai pensé que j'allais me coucher et dormir pendant douze heures.

[P. 1135]

Even though temporal rhythm is quite different in these two passages—chronological time-spans lengthen in the second one along with an increase and crescendo in syntactical tempo —they both remain disjunctive in the sense Sartre described. One event follows the other without causal connection, that is, although the second passage might be said to profit from its rhythmic momentum, passing from image to image until finally rising to the personalized, "ma joie quand," contrary to Sartre's view and albeit within a single sentence. An attentive reading of both texts reveals that, far from the unobtrusive narrator or even indifferent stranger he is accused of being, Meursault remains solidly present at the heart of his narration. Both styles originate within his single point of view, yet Meursault's expression, and therefore experience, differs drastically in these two passages. The first typifies his lucid attention to the moment replete with detailed events, and the second, his fatigued inattention spanning greater gaps of time by glimpses of widely disparate scenes and places. The two styles are not always as consistently separate as in these two examples, but often overlap or merge.[8]

On the other hand, Sartre's original contention that the *passé composé* constitutes, in fact, a present in *L'Étranger*, is essentially true.[9] By attenuating the esthetic tension between past experience and the present narrating of it, Camus succeeds in writing a story in the past tense—albeit a noun-centered past tense which seems to occur in the present. Yet, it is only partly through manipulating the tense of the verb that he succeeds in doing so. In addition, he exploits nonverbal expressions, some of which indicate the present, but most of which merely support the present in such a way as to constitute a false present in the Sartrean sense of *trompe-l'oeil*. Both work together, however, to create an overwhelming impression of immediacy. What remains to be determined more precisely is how Camus establishes and maintains this impression of immediacy throughout *L'Étranger* in view of the fact that the story is written predominantly in the past tense, and that the present appears in it infrequently and only by exception.[10]

### Meursault's *moi présent*

Meursault situates himself in the present in only two long passages of his story: the first opens the book, consisting of its first two paragraphs, and the second opens the last chapter of the book, consisting of only part of a paragraph.[11] The latter is followed by many more short insertions of Meursault's *moi présent* and sentences in the present tense than the first or than any other chapter of the book. This last chapter makes such a distinct impression, in fact, that some critics have declared it a third section of *L'Étranger*.[12] Its numerous present-tense sentences contribute an important element to its distinctive quality. In his curiously reductive, literal way, Robbe-Grillet will parody this specific technique of Camus by introducing his first-person narrator only at the beginning and end of *Dans le Labyrinthe*.

More important is Meursault's initial establishment of himself in the present tense, or his *moi présent* as the narrative voice which relates his own story from the sole point of view through which one has access to his experience and thus to the fictional world of the novel. The first two paragraphs of *L'Étranger*, written in the present and future tenses, establish Meursault not only as the narrator of his own story but also as contemporaneous with the narrated events.[13] The inital paragraph of *L'Étranger* is revealing in this respect:

> *Aujourd'hui maman est mort.* Ou peut-être hier, *je ne sais pas.* J'ai reçu un télegramme de l'asile: "Mère décédé. Enterrement demain. Sentiments distingués." *Cela ne veut rien dire.* C'était peut-être hier.        [P. 1125; italics mine]

The first word of the book, "aujourd'hui," indicates not only the immediacy of the event but also the narrator's contemporaneity with what is narrated. Today his mother has died and today he is telling about it. He foresees his trip to her wake and funeral in the next paragraph. But events subsequent to that, indeed events subsequent to the reception of the telegram, have not yet transpired. The third paragraph of *L'Étranger,* however, narrates Meursault's experience of his mother's wake and funeral in the past tense; the events have already occurred. This third paragraph is the actual beginning of Meursault's story, whereas the first two paragraphs must be considered in an introductory capacity only. "Aujourd'hui" occurs four times in Part 1 of *L'Étranger*, but only once in Part 2. Its frequency thus indicates precisely the temporal span of Part 1, while the temporal span of Part 2 always remains vague and approximate. The several insertions of "aujourd'hui" definitely indicate Meursault's presence and are strongly paralleled by similar temporal indicators not explicitly indicative of the present, but which create a false impression of the present.

"Je ne sais pas" is the second definite affirmation in this opening paragraph of Meursault's narrative self or of his *moi présent.* Arbitrary insertion of this phrase or similar ones in the present tense occurs more often in *L'Étranger* than any other technique to recall and to reassert continually Meursault's presence as narrator of his own story.

"Cela ne veut rien dire" is the last indication of Meursault's present thought in this first paragraph. It will be seen that phrases of this nature, although recounted in the present tense, generally introduce descriptions or maxims coined by Meursault which prove to be atemporal. They are true for all time and therefore not valid indications of any single moment present or past. The present tense in which they are related does not indicate Meursault's contemporaneity as a narrator.

Evident in the first paragraph of *L'Étranger*, therefore, are the three principal expressions, or temporal indicators, which Camus reiterates throughout *L'Étranger* in order continually to reestablish the presence of his narrator. Because the second of these three categories, "Je ne sais pas," appears most frequently and is the most definite indicator of Meursault's *moi présent*, I will discuss it first. Camus's use of "aujourd'hui" and similar expressions will then appear to be sometimes definitely indicating the present, sometimes creating a "false" present in order to enhance Camus's total esthetic effect. And finally, the temporal effect in *L'Étranger* of descriptions and maxims will be considered.

Besides indicating the three ways in which Camus establishes the present tense in *L'Étranger,* this first paragraph mixes past and present time in a way typical of Camus's entire text. After declaring affirmatively in the first sentence, "Today mother died," Meursault immediately appends an amendment conveying uncertainty as to the moment when this event occurred, "Or perhaps yesterday, I don't know," and by the end of the paragraph states the contrary to his first affirmation, "Perhaps it was yesterday." The temporal importance of events as well as this general temporal ambiguity is characteristic of Meursault's perspective in *L'Étranger*, and whether Camus studied this technique or developed it unconsciously is not as important as discovering its effect in the work as a whole.

Rather than present Meursault initially as the narrator of his story, and then plunge immediately into its past events to recount them chronologically as they occurred, Camus continually reaffirms Meursault's presence as narrator throughout the story. The constant interruptions of Meursault's actual presence create an illusory impression of immediacy. This illusory effect not only renders Meursault's tale more vivid by suggesting its continual unfolding in the present moment, but also, and more important, enhances the dramatic tension of *L'Étranger* by a continual vacillation between past and present leading up to the last chapter of the book in which past time seems to have caught up with present time just preceding Meursault's execution. But even here the impression is illusory. Resolution of this temporal problem is essential to Meursault's last crucial moments, yet in spite of his presence at the beginning of the last chapter and the continued reiteration of his presence throughout, even the last chapter is narrated predominantly in the past tense as having already occurred, so that the moment at which Meursault narrates his story with respect to his past remains enigmatic. But why this enigma, why this illusion? Meursault's story tends always toward the present in an ongoing flow which does not admit an end even at the last. These temporal vacillations in perspective add to the impression of life's triumph over death which Meursault experiences at the last in spite of his imminent demise.

## *Je ne sais pas*

Camus relies upon two principal ways of establishing the undeniable presence of his narrator. The first of these is the present, "je sais," "je crois," "je me souviens," "je peux dire," or the negative of such expressions by which Meursault inserts his present narrating "I" into the past events being narrated. There is no ambiguity of the *moi présent qui raconte* in these instances. Usually these expressions are inserted in the middle of the otherwise past-tense narrative in such a way that they do not attract attention.

*"Je ne sais pas* quel geste j'ai fait, mais il est resté debout derrière moi." [P. 1128; italics mine]
"Il faisait doux, le café m'avait rechauffé et par la porte ouverte entrait une odeur de nuit et de fleurs. *Je crois que* j'ai somnolé un peu." [P. 1129; italics mine]

The narrative unfolds without abrupt halt before these expressions of Meursault's *moi présent*. Both dramatic, or gestural, facts and descriptive facts are relayed without interrupting the narrative flow. In this sense, "je ne sais pas," or its equivalent is less abrupt than direct discourse with its typographical pauses, and thus favors the continuous narrative flow without interruption. On the other hand, these phrases might well be eliminated entirely; certainly if *L'Étranger* were written in the third person singular, they would have to be. But once eliminated, the urgency and immediacy of past events would disappear. A certain intimacy would be lost as well because, aside from their primarily temporal function, these expressions also personalize Meursault's narrative. Their frequency determines its impact.

Repetitions of such expressions in proximity subordinate the actual past context of events to a heightened impression of their present occurrence. Especially when such present-tense expressions occur in conjunction with nonverbal temporal expressions such as "maintenant" or "à présent" or "à un moment," they emphasize the *moi présent* by contrast to what was true in the past. On a single page, for example, three expressions of this nature in close proximity continually catch the narrative up into the present perspective:

J'avais même l'impression que cette morte, couchée au milieu d'eux, ne signifiait rien à leurs yeux. Mais *je crois maintenant* que c'était une impression fausse.
Nous avons tous pris du café, servi par le concierge. Ensuite, *je ne sais plus*. La nuit a passé. *Je me souviens* qu'à un moment, j'ai ouvert les yeux et j'ai vu que les vieillards dormaient tassés sur eux-mêmes. . . . [P. 1130–31; italics mine]

Without these italicized present-tense expressions, this passage could very well be read as a continuous past, but their constant reiteration and interruption impart to the entire passage the immediacy and the solidity of the contemporary witness. In this sense, Meursault not only continually ratifies his experience, but also continually witnesses his own story as if pleading his case from beginning to end.[14]

The uncertainty of the content in these expressions creates an illusion of not knowing the outcome of the narrative. Because of Meursault's lack of certainty the plot seems to be continually unfolding. Events which, in fact, belong to Meursault's past seem to occur at present: *"Je ne sais pas* pourquoi cela a fait rire Marie. *Je crois qu'*elle avait un peu trop bu" (p. 1161). Marie seems to be laughing and drinking with Meursault as he speaks of her.

In addition, an air of honesty is lent to Meursault's expression by his continual attempts at exactitude. "J'ai répondu, *je ne sais pas encore pourquoi, que j'ignorais jusqu'ici qu'on me jugeât mal à cet égard . . ."* (p. 1157). Continually rectifying his attitude, Meursault always seems to be searching for the *mot juste.* That he remembers some events but not others, that he interprets them somewhat differently at present than he has done in the past, imparts an undeniable authenticity to Meursault's expression. Whether Meursault judges in retrospect, or interprets in retrospect, the past event he is recounting, he transforms it into a present event by his very act of judgment or of interpretation.

In the remembrance of past events, Meursault sometimes struggles with their expression until they seem to erupt dramatically into the present. During his trial in particular, when Meursault meets the silence of the courtroom at the moment of his sentence, Camus makes use of this dramatic effect. Meursault hesitates and struggles with his present expression in the attempt to render precisely his experience of the momentary silence in the courtroom which overwhelmed him: *"Je crois bien* que c'était de la considération" (p. 1199). His conclusion solidifies and vivifies his experience, eternalizing this event because of its participation in both past and present. Later also, introducing his encounter with the priest, Meursault's present expression, although parenthetical and not dramatic in itself, introduces his memory of the violence of the past drama into present awareness: "*Alors, je ne sais pas pourquoi,* il y a quelque chose qui a crevé en moi" (p. 1208). Sometimes these phrases serve as bridges in time or action. They are transitional in nature in such cases, and, as in the former passage containing three such expressions in close proximity, bridge temporal lapses so that they are never filled with another point of view. Perspective thus remains unified. In this sense, they do not partake of drama, but remain a purely transitional technique and one which favors the smooth flow of Meursault's narrative. "*Je crois que* j'ai dormi parce que me suis réveillé avec des étoiles sur le visage" (p. 1209).

## Aujourd'hui

Indicating the present with equal certainty are the several instances of "aujourd'hui" which recur most frequently in Part 1 of *L'Étranger*, and only once in Part 2. To note these present moments, Meursault, as narrator, would seem to be present at the beginning and sometimes in the middle of each chapter in Part 1. Chapters 1, 2, 3, and 4, that is, attest his presence, though not chapters 5 and 6, which are entirely remembered or recounted in the past. The sequence and frequency of these notations indicate that Meursault probably writes down or narrates his story at the end of each day in Part 1.[15] The duration of all events in Part 1 does not surpass three weeks, as the following outline indicates.

| | | |
|---|---|---|
| Jeudi: wake | 1. | "*Aujourd'hui,* maman est morte." [P. 1125] |
| Vendredi | | "*Aujourd'hui,* le soleil débordant qui faisait tressaillir le paysage le rendait inhumain et déprimant." [P. 1133] |
| Samedi: Marie | 2. | "En me réveillant, j'ai compris pourquoi mon |
| Dimanche | | patron avait l'air mécontent quand je lui ai demandé mes deux jours de congé: *c'est aujourd'hui samedi.*" [P. 1136] |

| | |
|---|---|
| Lundi | 3. *"Aujourd'hui* j'ai beaucoup travaillé au bureau." [P. 1141] |
| Samedi | 4. *"Hier,* c'était samedi et Marie est venue comme nous en étions convenus." |
| Dimanche | *"Ce matin,* Marie est restée et je lui ai dit que nous déjeunerions ensemble." [P. 1149] |
| | 5. No indication of time. |
| Dimanche | 6. No indication of time except *"Le dimanche,* j'ai eu de la peine à me réveiller et il a . . ."  [P. 1158; italics mine] |

In chapters 5 and 6 time is less important than event. "Le dimanche" could indicate any Sunday, but probably indicates the weekend following the last Sunday explicitly mentioned in chapter 4. The scene of the murder becomes all-important in these last two chapters, so that chronological sequence narrows to narrative event, or gives way before the depth of experience. The murder of the Arab becomes a totality of experience in which time is absent except as the still moment of noon under the blazing heat of the sun. Elemental forces of a cosmic and symbolic nature transfix in spatial configuration the series of events which constitute a single narrative moment.

In this first part Meursault seems to relate, to note down, or at least to remember his story as it happens from day to day, just as one might write a diary at the end of each day. "Today I did this," constitutes the unit of duration he either normally chooses or is normally able to relate. He does not know what will occur, there is no future tense, and he notes only what has happened within a single day in the past tense. That each chapter ends with nightfall is significant in this respect. It adds to the impression that each chapter occurs during daylight hours and that Meursault ends the day by retelling, by writing in his diary, or at least by remembering the events of the day just before sleep. It is pertinent to recall at this point the schematic day of which *L'Étranger* is composed in its entirety. Meursault's mother is buried in the

morning, the Arab is killed at noon, and Meursault's last
scene with the priest takes place at night.[16]

The only single instance in which "aujourd'hui" appears
in Part 2 of *L'Étranger* is in the last chapter. The priest says
to Meursault, "Mais vous mourrez plus tard si vous ne mourez
pas *aujourd'hui*" (p. 1206). This is the only indication of
Meursault's presence as a narrator during his narration of
Part 2. That Camus changed the last word of this sentence
from "bientôt" to "aujourd'hui" indicates at least that he
wanted Meursault's death to be imminent if not on the very
day on which he relates this last chapter of his narrative.[17]

Meursault's *prise de conscience* with which Part 2 is primarily concerned inhibits specific chronological sequence, and,
although greater spans of time are noted by Meursault at
various intervals—five months, eleven months, twelve months
—no precise time sequence can be deduced from these references. Tempo is indeed slower in Part 2, and Camus's division
of chapters into topical units rather than chronological sequence inhibits further chronological presentation or development of events.[18] Not until the last chapter of the book takes
place on Meursault's last day does present time play a role
in Part 2 of *L'Étranger*. The chronological sense of time belongs to the external events of Meursault's daily life, whereas
the mosaic which groups events topically belongs to Meursault's internal *prise de conscience*.


## Camus's trompe-l'oeil


Much more numerous than these few instances of "aujour-
d'hui" which indicate a real present, are other temporal indicators such as "à ce moment," "à présent," or "maintenant,"
which lend urgency to past events, creating a false present, or
giving the illusion of a present. The instantaneous significance
of these expressions plays perhaps the greatest role in their
creation of a false present, but again the number of times they

appear adds to their effectiveness. Although they occur less frequently with a verb in the present, "je ne sais pas à présent" or "je crois maintenant," for example, they do in such cases constitute an actual present. It may be that they somehow extend and carry over their present significance when occurring alone in the sole context of the past narrative. But more likely their significance and their frequency play the major roles in creating such an unavoidable sense of immediacy and of momentary urgency that the past indeed seems to be present.

In this sense most expressions containing the explicit word "moment," such as "à ce moment," "pour le moment," "au bout d'un moment," "à partir de ce moment," "à un moment," "un moment après," along with "maintenant," "à présent," and "alors," convey more urgency and rapidity than "ensuite," "peu après," "le lendemain," or "le soir."

The following sentences are typical of Meursault's expression in Part 1 and seem most often to introduce displacement of persons or of things in the dramatic mode rather than the descriptive.

"*A ce moment,* le concierge est entré derrière mon dos. . . . *A ce moment,* le concierge m'a dit . . ."          [P. 1127]

"*C'est à ce moment,* que les amis de maman sont entrés."
          [P. 1129]

"*A ce moment,* un camion est arrivé dans un fracas. . . ."
          [P. 1141; italics mine]

"Maintenant," on the other hand, appears more frequently in descriptions, and often seems to mean "now" in the present as well as "now" in the past, although nominally it refers only to past events. Meursault again seems to be present at the moment he is narrating, or rather to bring the past narrative up to his present narration of it, rendering the whole more concrete and more vivid.

"L'un des hommes qui entouraient la voiture s'était laissé dépasser aussi et marchait *maintenant* à mon niveau."          [P. 1133]

"*Maintenant* il est trop grand pour moi."          [P. 1137]

"Il a ajouté que, pourtant, c'était *maintenant* une histoire finie."
[P. 1159]

"Nous avons marché longtemps sur la plage. Le soleil était *maintenant* écrasant."                                    [P. 1163; italics mine]

If one compares these expressions with notations of time which are equally frequent in Part 2, the more urgent and immediate effect of those already cited in Part 1 becomes at once evident:

"*Tout de suite après* mon arrestation, j'ai été interrogé plusieurs fois. . . . *Huit jours après,* le juge d'instruction m'a regardé avec curiosité. . . . *Au début,* je ne l'ai pas pris au sérieux." [P. 1169]

"*Le lendemain, un* avocat est venu me voir à la prison. . . . *Peu de temps après,* j'étais conduit de nouveau devant le juge d'instruction."                                                   [Pp. 1170–71]

"*Après un silence,* il s'est levé et m'a dit qu'il voulait m'aider. . . ."
"*Par la suite . . .*"                           [P. 1174; all italics mine]

These passages are all taken from chapter 1 of Part 2, and the longer duration of time or the vaguer reference tends to slow the tempo considerably.

By far the largest number of notations by Meursault made in the present tense belong to one of two categories, both of which eliminate his presence as narrator. These take the form of either descriptions or maxims, which are atemporal, and therefore belong completely neither to the past events nor to the present narration of those events. Rather, they share in both tenses and serve to join past to present in a single atemporal moment which generalizes their content, pulls it out of chronological sequence, and transcends any specific historical or chronological context.

## Descriptions

In three precise and prolonged descriptions, Meursault presents his room, his neighbor Salamano, and his friend and second neighbor Sintès in the present tense. Camus's reasons for these present descriptions are not evident, since other secondary characters such as Marie, Céleste, Thomas Pérez, or the legal and religious representatives in *L'Étranger* are equally important, sometimes even more important to the novel as a whole and to Meursault as its protagonist. Still, these three long descriptions stand in the present tense and are representative of other descriptive clauses scattered throughout the book, but which occur singly rather than in passages of any length.

Nominally, these descriptions might be classified as what Grevisse has termed a "présent pittoresque." The present used in this sense refers to atemporal facts which are true at all times, or which continue from past to present.[19]

In the first description of this nature, Meursault mixes past and present tenses in describing the room in which he lives at the time of narrating his story, and in which he has lived during the narrated past, and even further back in the past to a time preceding the narrative when his mother still lived with him. The curious mixture of past and present tenses in this description is instructive with regard to Camus's total temporal effect in *L'Étranger*.

Meursault relates the following description in his flat factual style uncolored at this point by emotional strain. Events remain in the past from which he takes his point of departure. Description, however, is related in the present. The presence or absence of Meursault in the room at the moment of narration remains undetermined.

Après le déjeuner, je me suis ennuyé un peu et j'ai erré dans l'appartement. [Il était commode quand maman était là. *Maintenant il est* trop grand pour moi et j'ai dû transporter dans ma chambre la table de la salle à manger. Je ne *vis* plus que dans cette pièce, entre les chaises de paille un peu creusées, l'armoire dont la glace *est* jaunie, la table de toilette et le lit de cuivre. Les reste *est* à l'abandon.] Un peu plus tard, pour faire quelque chose, j'ai pris un vieux journal et je l'ai lu. J'y ai découpé une réclame des sels Kruschen et je l'ai collée dans un vieux cahier ou je *mets* les choses qui m'*amusent* dans les journaux. Je me suis aussi lavé les mains et, pour finir, je me suis mis au balcon.

Ma chambre *donne* sur la rue principale de faubourg.
L'aprés-midi était beau. . . . Derrière eux, une mère énorme, en
robe de soie marron, et le père, un petit homme assez frêle que je
*connais* de vue . . . Le ciel était pur mais sans éclat au-dessus des
ficus qui *bordent* la rue.                    [P. 1138; italics mine]

Each of the present-tense verbs italicized in this passage
could be written in a past tense if Meursault were merely relating his story. Their contrast with past-tense verbs effects a
kind of tension which casts the scene in an atemporal moment.
The scene transcends the moment so that the reality of Meursault's apartment and the description of its contents are finally
more striking, more concrete, and of a separate solidity related
neither to past nor to present. The frequent change of verbal
tense renders Meursault's presence in the room uncertain.
Such present-tense verbs which describe tend to eliminate the
narrator's presence. External perceptions such as these are not
temporal indicators although written in the present tense. The
picturesque quality, if we are to translate Grevisse's title literally, is emphasized here rather than the temporal. The spatial
scene, that is, its solidity, its reality, and its durability beyond
any present moment is Camus's emphasis here, not Meursault's presence as either his *moi présent* or his *moi passé*.


## Maxims

Descriptions deal primarily with external perceptions on Meursault's part. The second category of statements he makes in
the present, but which do not serve as temporal indicators,
includes maxims, or general truths which reflect inner conviction rather than describe outer reality. This general category is
also atemporal and is best defined by Grevisse as the "présent
gnomique."[20]

The preponderance of these maxims in the second part of
*L'Étranger* corresponds to the deepening of Meursault's critical
and interpretative faculties or to the discoveries of his intellect.

When his sensual faculties are limited by his imprisonment, Meursault's intellect exercises itself more freely. When Meursault's vision is imprisoned, it "goes underground," or deepens his insight instead of remaining acutely aware of external stimuli. Acoustics in particular, and his tactile sense, replace his hyperacute vision of the first part.

The majority of such maxims in Part 1 of *L'Étranger* refer to specific truths personal to Meursault, which most often describe his simple delights in life. This type of maxim does not in any sense posit a temporal present, but rather, an atemporal truth which exists above, beyond, or beside the temporal. These initial expressions depend almost exclusively upon the word "aimer."

"Comme *j'aime* beaucoup le café au lait . . ."

[P. 1128; italics mine]

"J'ai pensé que c'était dimanche et cela m'a ennuyé: je n'*aime* pas le dimanche." [P. 1137; italics mine]

"Il voulait ensuite aller au bordel, mais j'ai dit non parce que je n'*aime* pas ça." [P. 1151; italics mine]

Later, in Part 2, Meursault's expression becomes more profound during his imprisonment: "D'ailleurs, *je dois reconnaître que* l'intérêt qu'on *trouve* à occuper les gens ne *dure* pas longtemps" (p. 1193). Or again, "Non, il n'y avait pas d'issue et *personne ne peut imaginer* ce que sont les soirs dans les prisons" (p. 1181).

The last chapter of *L'Étranger* abounds in such general statements, which, at this point in Meursault's awareness, constitute impersonal maxims applicable to humanity at large. These profound statements are indicative of Meursault's attempt to "understand" life and death in such a way as to reconcile the two. Their extension and general application to humanity at large make of Meursault at the last the moralist that Camus was.

"Mais, naturellement, on *ne peut pas* être toujours raisonnable."

[P. 1201]

"Maman disait souvent qu'on n'*est* jamais tout à fait mal-
heureux."                                                    [P. 1203]

"Mais tout le monde *sait* que la vie ne *vaut* pas la peine d'être
vécue. Dans le fond, je n'ignorais pas que mourir à trente ans ou
à soixante-dix ans *importe* peu puisque, naturellement, dans les
deux cas, d'autres hommes et d'autres femmes vivront, et cela pendant des milliers d'années."                                  [P. 1204]

"Du moment qu'on *meurt,* comment et quand, cela *n'importe* pas,
c'était évident."                           [P. 1204; all italics mine]

In Part 1, generalities derive primarily from Meursault's
personal experience, from his likes and dislikes of specific external situations, but they develop gradually in Part 2 into
maxims on human behavior dear to the French moralist tradition, and finally, in the last chapter, convey primarily the reconciliation in Meursault of life to death. The present tense
in these expressions does not designate any temporal mode,
but does impress Meursault's convictions upon us more concretely because they reflect his newly acquired profundity.
There is indeed a great difference of profundity between the
Meursault who proclaims, "J'*aime* le café," in the first chapter,
and the Meursault who discovers, or at least declares, in the
last, "Tout le monde *sait* que la vie ne *vaut* pas la peine d'être
vécue."

The subtle irony contained in expressions such as "tout
le monde sait que" or "je n'ignorais pas que" or "naturellement" or "c'était évident" is that they suggest the contrary of
what they state, so that often Meursault's maxims must be
understood by negative application. Their esthetic effect stems
not only from the more evident, overt mental struggle between
the upsurge of life in the face of certain death, but also from
Meursault's emotions torn between hope and resignation, and
even more intimately and tellingly from his final affirmations
of resignation.

Everything he designates as "evident" or "natural" quali-
fies what he states by casting doubt on its evidence or natural-
ness. Although this technique is traditional in French literature, dating at least from Molière's "sans doute," it is a stylis-

tic device sparsely used by Camus in contrast to Robbe-Grillet, who literally writes entire passages in the negative which must be ultimately understood by the reader in the affirmative.

## Direct quotation

Finally, Camus's rare use of direct quotation introduces a sense of urgency and immediacy into his past narrative, thus creating another kind of false present. All direct quotations in *L'Étranger* are made by others who address Meursault.[21] When they appear, as in Meursault's conversations with the dignitaries of the rest home, or later during his trial and especially during his last conversation with the priest, his story at these points again seems to take place in the present although such statements belong to his past narrative. Meursault remembers verbatim the words of others in these scenes, thus rendering them vividly dramatic as well as concretely present. By contrast, his own responses are normally related in indirect discourse or restricted to a short yes or no answer. Often his response is not verbal at all, as in Marie's visit with him in prison, but the scene remains nevertheless dramatic and immediate because of the direct quotation of others' comments interspersed with Meursault's own monosyllabic responses and more lengthy descriptions in indirect discourse of his impressions. The scene of Marie's visit might fruitfully be compared to the famous "comices agricoles" in *Madame Bovary* for its incorporation of the words and actions of others to substantiate and to dramatize the rapport between Meursault and Marie. T. S. Eliot's objective correlative again obtains in both these scenes as the best way of understanding and interpreting them.

Camus does not avail himself of similar support from surrounding voices in the final scene between Meursault and the priest, however, but here again dramatizes principally by quoting the priest verbatim and by allowing Meursault to express himself primarily in indirect discourse. At the climax of this scene where Meursault cries out to the priest his accep-

tance and justification of his life as he has lived it, Camus
neither places Meursault's assertions between quotation marks
nor does he report them in the present tense.[22] If he had done
so, the scene might have become even more vivid. Leaving it in
indirect discourse and in the past tense retains Meursault's
point of view as witness to his story in the present and as actor
only in the past.

Thus, it is clear that Camus distinguishes until the very
last the past action of Meursault's narrative from his present
witnessing of it. Meursault's present perspective, however, continually determines the point of view through which the reader
has access to the events of his past narrative. The reader is
always viewing the past narrative from a present perspective,
therefore, which never allows the past to overtake it. The diffi-
culty for the critic is to establish the present moment or moments of narration of *L'Étranger* with respect to its past narrative.[23] Though Camus limits his narrative events to the past
and his perspective to the present, he manipulates both in such
a way as to create a continually unfolding present, precisely as
Sartre later prescribed.

Obviously, Camus does not render Sartrean precepts literal
on the temporal plane by a sole use of the present tense as will
be true in the New Novel. But Camus does make every
effort to transform the past into an ever-unfolding present
and, in the process, creates a temporal ambiguity which favors
always the narrating *moi présent* over the acting, participating
*moi passé*. With regard to this highly conscious, contrived
aspect of Camus's art, J. Cruickshank justly comments:
"Camus, like many of his contemporaries, uses a highly intel-
lectualized artistic medium in order to convey a direct and
un-intellectualized impression of human experience."[24]

## Manipulation of person

The adoption of the first person in *L'Étranger* renders author
intervention extremely difficult, if not impossible. Theoreti-

cally, the author cannot intervene in a flagrant manner or even in the subtle manner of Sartre, who does so by taking advantage of the third person. Practically, however, there are certain moments at which Meursault expresses himself in a way incongruous with his general nature, and moments, especially at the last, during which he expresses himself with such profundity that one cannot avoid assigning many of these thoughts, in part at least, to Camus.

If one accepts the generally held thesis that Camus's first person represents in fact a third person, however, it is not difficult to ascertain in *L'Étranger* the same ambiguity which exists in *L'Enfance d'un chef* between the author and his point-of-view-subjectivity. By conceiving his first person as a third person, Camus is quite as able as Sartre to profit from the technique of narrated monologue, or *discours indirect libre*, in spite of literary convention confining this technique purely to third-person narratives. This technique has the dual advantage of eliminating the author's overt presence within his fictional universe in the form of nonsituated comments, but of including him through the comments of his protagonist, who is firmly anchored within the fictional universe. Lucien and Meursault do not speak always for themselves alone but also include thoughts clearly attributable to their respective authors. Even while throwing the author's voice out the front door in theory, therefore, both Sartre and Camus creep back into their works through their protagonist's voices. In so doing, they fulfill Percy Lubbock's original theory of fictional perspective which opted for the third person in order to include the author's ideas within the single point of view of his protagonist, even though they contradict the contemporary trend —and Sartre's theory—of limiting point of view to a single protagonist in order to *exclude* the author's voice.[25]

Many incongruities in Meursault's expression can be ascribed to this central ambiguity between the author and his protagonist, while many others derive from an ambiguity between Meursault and other fictional characters: in particular, his various prosecutors during the trial scenes. Although seem-

ing to remain solidly centered within his protagonist, Camus
subjects him to an entire spectrum of perspectives encompassing everything from a rather primitive Voltairean naïveté to
the highly developed sophistication of Camus's own moralizing
voice. In this respect, B. T. Fitch correctly noted that once
the reader has been made to identify with Meursault and,
literally, to live in his skin during the assassination scene,
nothing can convince him thereafter of Meursault's guilt.[26]
Camus is freed thereby to take every liberty with Meursault
throughout Part 2 without unduly taxing the reader's empathy.

Other incongruities in Meursault's expression can be ascribed, not to an ambiguity between the author and his protagonist, nor even to the ambiguity between Meursault and his
prosecutors, but to an ambiguity between Meursault's *moi
présent* and his *moi passé*. This derives partly from his establishing the reader in the perspective of the narrator (*moi
présent*) rather than in that of the hero (*moi passé*). In addition, a few of Meursault's expressions stand so patently out of
context that they break out of the fictional field altogether.

Camus's manipulation of the first person in *L'Étranger*,
therefore, creates multiple ambiguities in perspective which
fall generally within the following three categories: first, the
ambiguities fostered by Meursault's undue naïveté; second,
those derived from Meursault's lyrical or profound expressions; and finally, ambiguities inherent in the hiatus between
Meursault's narrating *moi présent* and his participating *moi
passé*. Although I will discuss each category by turn, it is clear
that a number of these ambiguities subtly overlap.


### Irony: Meursault's naïveté


The most obvious way in which Camus intervenes by manipulating his characters occurs during his most blatant satirical
scenes: the first, between Meursault and the *juge d'instruction*,
and the second, between Meursault and the prosecutor. In

these scenes the characters, in particular Meursault, express themselves so naïvely that the presence of the author becomes manifest.

Camus's empathetic portrayal of Meursault in the last chapter of Part 1 of *L'Étranger* leaves the reader quite unprepared for the ironical mode which opens Part 2, in which both the judge and Meursault display a naïveté too great to remain credible. Both Meursault's naïveté and that of the judge are suggested from the beginning. When informed that the state will supply his lawyer, for example, Meursault responds naïvely: "J'ai trouvé qu'il était très commode que la justice se chargeât de ces détails. Je le lui ai dit. Il m'a approuvé et a conclu que la loi était bien faite" (p. 1169). Although the judge's simplicity is not initially as apparent as is Meursault's, both characters are presented eventually as equally naïve in the dramatic exchange which takes place between them; Camus is particularly adept at portraying the ironic naïveté of their gestures. Nominally, point of view remains with Meursault, through whose vision and interpretation events are disclosed, but both Meursault and the judge are equidistant from the reader in this opening scene. Meursault recedes from the foreground, taking part almost exclusively in his fictional environment; he becomes more actor than spectator, thus distancing his perspective from the reader.

Perspective falters and loses its firm center when Meursault preoccupies himself with the social gesture which has so far remained entirely alien to him. Unduly credulous, for example, Meursault remembers first taking leave of the judge: "En sortant j'allais même lui tendre la main, mais je me suis souvenu à temps que j'avais tué un homme" (p. 1169). Camus, like Sartre, creates an ironic breach in Meursault's perspective by causing his protagonist to exclaim too often that he is exactly like "tout le monde," or that he loves his mother "comme tout le monde" (pp. 1171–72). In this as in other expressions frequently reiterated, like "Je n'aurais pas dû dire cela," or "Ça ne voulait rien dire," Meursault does indeed protest too much for his word to be literally accepted by the reader, particularly upon rereading *L'Étranger.* The judge draws his share of ridicule and satire both as legal and religious counsellor. Legally, he not only presumes but also exaggerates Meursault's moral guilt in the compulsive precision of his questioning as reported by Meursault verbatim: "Pourquoi avez-vous attendu entre le premier et le second coup? . . . Pourquoi, pourquoi avez-vous tiré sur un corps à terre?" (p. 1172). Camus's ironic portrait of legal and religious justice climaxes in the judge's rabid protests while waving a crucifix before Meursault's eyes:

"Voulez-vous que ma vie n'ait pas de sens? . . . Moi, je suis chrétien. Je demande pardon de tes fautes à celui-là. Comment peux-tu ne pas croire qu'il a souffert pour toi?"          [P. 1173]

Meursault's continual silence in response to such outrage as well as his naïve acceptance without comment of such a scene links him closely to his executioner. At first blush, this effect might seem to derive from Camus's avowed purpose of quoting others verbatim but never his protagonist, except for the fact that in his final interpretation of this stage of his pretrial, Meursault's perspective literally seems to merge with that of the rabid judge. All would truly seem for the best in the best of possible worlds for Meursault at the end of his year-long series of interviews with this *juge d'instruction* as interpreted in the following words:[27]

Personne, en ces heures-là, n'était méchant avec moi. Tout était si naturel, si bien réglé et si sobrement joué que j'avais l'impression ridicule de "faire partie de la famille." Et au bout des onze mois qu'a duré cette instruction je peux dire que je m'étonnais presque de n'être jamais réjoui d'autre chose que de ces rares instants où le juge me reconduisait à la porte de son cabinet en me frappant sur l'épaule et en me disant d'un air cordial: C'est fini pour aujourd'hui, monsieur l'Antéchrist."          [P. 1174]

The second scene in which Camus similarly satirizes Meursault's naïveté occurs in the courtroom during the prosecutor's accusation. During the prosecutor's entire grotesque

distortion of the events of his crime, Meursault allies himself
with his accuser by his naïve approbation:

"J'ai trouvé que sa façon de voir les événements ne manquait pas
de clarté. Ce qu'il disait était plausible."                    [P.1194]

As the prosecuting attorney continues his crushing accusation, eliminating even the remotest possibility of Meursault's innocence, Meursault accepts his condemnation in his
own naïvely distorted fashion.

Sans doute, je ne pouvais pas m'empêcher de reconnaître qu'il
avait raison. Je ne regrettais pas beaucoup mon acte. Mais tant
d'acharnement m'étonnait. J'aurais voulu essayer de lui expliquer
cordialement, presque avec affection, que je n'avais jamais pu
regretter vraiment quelque chose. J'étais toujours pris par ce qui
allait arriver, par aujourd'hui ou par demain.                  [Pp. 1194–95]

Meursault's express desire to have explained his actions
"cordially" to the prosecuting attorney, followed by his re-
straint from doing so, is typical of his passivity and naïve good
will in all the legal scenes. Exaggeration of these characteristics
throughout his trial damns Meursault quite as effectively as
do the same traits in Voltaire's Candide or Sartre's Lucien.

Finally, during a climactic moment of the prosecutor's
accusation, as in the initial scene with the judge, Mersault's
point of view mingles with and joins that of the prosecuting
attorney. But this time Camus dispenses with quotation marks
even though Meursault reports the attorney's words verbatim,
with the effect that Meursault's very existence becomes evanescent; he is present only as a vehicle through which flow
the prosecutor's words.

Il disait qu'il était penché sur elle [mon âme] et qu'il n'avait
rien trouvé, Messieurs les jurés. Il disait qu'à la vérité, je n'en
avais point d'âme, et que rien d'humain, et pas un des principes
moraux qui gardent le coeur des hommes ne m'était accessible,
"Sans doute, ajoutait-il, nous ne saurions le lui reprocher."
                                                                 [P. 1195]

Using the imperfect tense to cite the prosecutor directly
without quotation marks makes the distinct impression of

direct discourse here, especially because of the direct address, "Messieurs les jurés." Even though Meursault reports the prosecutor's speech indirectly, their opposing viewpoints seem to merge.

From this series of examples it is clear that whenever Meursault identifies and allies himself so closely with another speaker in *L'Étranger* that his account reports the latter's words verbatim, albeit in indirect discourse, Meursault's point of view momentarily is submerged under the dominant tirade of the other. Often introduced by "selon lui" and followed by the imperfect tense, this technique steadily builds ironic tension until it climaxes dramatically by its frequency in the trial scenes. Meursault's expression in these scenes extends from a naïve acceptance of all the accusations made against him to a merging of his own point of view with that of his prosecutors.

B. T. Fitch's interpretation of this precise use of *discours indirect libre* in *L'Étranger* is by far the most just and the most telling with respect to Camus's art. At the same time, M. Fitch's description can be applied precisely to Sartre's similar manipulation of *discours indirect libre* in the case of Lucien surreptitiously introducing his "je" into his third-person narrative. In the cases of both Sartre and Camus, the "je" introduced represents the perspective of "the other" or of "others" whose perspective the protagonist temporarily assumes.

Nous y avons le cas curieux d'un "je" qui se rapporte au narrateur sans nous donner pour cela son propre point de vue sur lui-même, qui nous donne, au contraire, le point de vue d'autrui. . . . En changeant le "il" de l'avocat pour un "je" sans mettre le "je" dans le contexte du discours indirect explicite, Meursault paraît assumer en quelque sorte l'interprétation des événements formulée par l'avocat. . . . [Cette technique] fournit un véhicule discret mais efficace de l'ironie et de l'ambiguité.[28]

Meursault only begins to see himself through the eyes of these "others" in Part 2 of *L'Étranger* and thus begins to escape for the first time from his "égocentrisme naturel et irréfléchi," according to M. Fitch.

Further, M. A. Abbou directly relates the specific impact of this use of *discours indirect libre* within the fictional world between two subjectivity-points-of-view to the same impact on the reader in the outside world between himself and the fiction:

Ainsi, si, à l'intérieur de l'univers romanesque, Meursault se trouve réduit à zéro par le fait que les avocats se substituent à lui, sur le plan de la création romanesque et des rapports du lecteur avec cet univers, ce sont les avocats qui sont réduits à zéro.[29]

Indeed, there is no way of escaping Camus's ambiguities or his irony written quite deliberately into these scenes. Ambiguous statements, such as those cited in the trial scenes, which can be attributed at once either to the narrator or to the judge or prosecutor, correspond precisely to those found in Robbe-Grillet's *Dans le Labyrinthe*. But Robbe-Grillet literally multiplies this kind of ambiguity to the point of utter confusion, without leaving the remotest possibility of untangling the various knots or of solving the numerous riddles of who is speaking, where and when. Camus employs pointedly a technique which is later compounded into utter confusion by Robbe-Grillet.

## Meursault's lyrical expressions

Beside Meursault's naïve expressions, which sometimes eclipse his point of view, stand his lyrical ones, which very often seem alien to him in a different way. Although Meursault's lyricism has generally been recognized as only one of his two styles of expression, the following two quotations, taken from the first part of *L'Étranger*, might be considered examples of an emotional intensity and a lyrical pitch reached by Meursault quite untypical of him. Accompanying his mother's coffin to her grave, Meursault forms the following tableau from fatigue, emotion, sun and a combination of nearly all his senses, dominated as usual by his hyperacute vision.

J'etais un peu perdu entre le ciel bleu et blanc et la monotonie
de ces couleurs, noir gluant du goudron ouvert, noir terne des
habits, noir laqué de la voiture. Tout cela, l'odeur de cuir et de
crottin de la voiture, celle du vernis et celle de l'encens, la
fatigue d'une nuit d'insomnie, me troublait le regard et les idées.
[P. 1134]

The repetition of certain sounds like "peu perdu . . . ciel
bleu et blanc . . . monotonie . . . couleurs" leads up to the poetic
description "noir gluant du goudron ouvert" in which the
liquid sounds of *l*'s and *r*'s and the rhythm of the words precisely embody their content. Further sonorities, parallel
rhythms and constructions, lend an unaccustomed finesse to
Meursault's expression. The link between Meursault's "regard" and his "idées" remains constant in *L'Étranger*, so that
"seeing" most often precedes or accompanies, and sometimes
even signifies, "knowing" or "understanding" as in this passage. The primacy of Meursault's visual and other senses is
not curtailed until his imprisonment, where the awakening of
his intellectual consciousness adds a moral or philosophical
dimension to his lyrical statements.

A second and much-discussed example in which Meursault's poetic expression overwhelms his normally limited
speech occurs just preceding his murder of the Arab. In the
following sentence not only the sonorities and rhythms, but
also the tripartite structure convey a more poetic turn of mind
than usual in Meursault. As a tribute to Camus's genius, this
single sentence crystallizes Meursault's total sentiment into a
small masterpiece of lyrical expression:

"J'avais envie de retrouver le murmure de son eau, envie de fuir
le soleil, l'effort et les pleurs de femmes, envie enfin de retrouver
l'ombre et son repos."                                    [P. 1165]

The nuance and the finesse of expressions such as these
poetize Meursault's normal speech patterns so that, when too
perfect, they clash with his accustomed rhythm and stand out
of context. Generally, critics agree that Meursault is incapa-
ble of such lyrical expression. Lyrical passages in *L'Étranger*,
nevertheless, are usually considered to express Meursault's

total coincidence with his sensations. Because such lyricism surpasses Meursault's usual powers of expression, most critics interpret it as Camus's voice: "Camus a exprimé ce que sentait son héros sous une forme dont ce dernier se serait servi s'il en avait été capable."[30] Moreover, Sartre had originally hinted at his awareness of a lyrical mode of expression in Meursault which he, too, attributed to Camus's own personal expression: "A travers le récit essoufflé de Meursault, j'aperçois en transparence une prose poétique plus large qui le sous-tend et qui doit être le mode d'expression personnel de M. Camus."[31]

More strikingly incongruous with Meursault's general mode of expression than his lyrical exaggerations and yet partaking of this same lyricism are the last sentences in Parts 1 and 2 of *L'Étranger*, which serve as résumés of all that has preceded. Not only incongruous with Meursault's mode of expression but also with his mode of thought, these two statements patently break out of context by their overwritten and contrived form.

The author's presence is inescapable in the last sentence of Part 1 because of its sudden and grossly drawn metaphor: "Et c'était comme quatre coups brefs que je frappais sur la porte du malheur" (p. 1166). Although it presumably serves a transitional function between the two divisions of *L'Étranger*, introducing Meursault's contemplative mood of Part 2, its sense of prediction, of impending doom, and of clairvoyance is totally alien to Meursault.[32] Meursault's sentiment is more finely and more originally expressed, and keeps more closely within the fictional *données* of this central scene in his preceding statement: "J'ai compris que j'avais détruit l'équilibre du jour, le silence exceptionnel d'une plage où j'avais été heureux" (p. 1166). In order to remain consonant with the Meursault delineated up to this point, Camus would have done well to have left it at that.

Again, the very last sentence of *L'Étranger* reveals the too-heavy hand of its author in a statement attributed to Meursault which lacks all verisimilitude:

"Pour que tout soit consommé, pour que je me sente moins seul, il me restait à souhaiter qu'il y ait beaucoup de spectateurs le jour de mon éxécution et qu'ils m'accueillent avec des cris de haine."

[P. 1210]

In addition to its too-facile parallel with the martyred Christ, this statement expresses Meursault's paradoxical desire of a fraternal bond at the moment when all bonds are broken. That this bond be the negative one of hate condemns humanity to a single and seemingly unwarranted emotion with respect to Meursault, whose death results from misunderstanding rather than from hate. Meursault has just vindicated his life, moreover, and subsequently experienced a joy in living which derives from, as well as transcends, all temporal accidents of existence. He has just "opened" himself to the world for the first time in a spirit of fraternal love which belies the shock of hate and of martrydom expressed in this last statement. The imagined gesture is belittling and too dramatic for Meursault. The esthetic shock afforded by such an inconsistent statement weakens Meursault's story at its close with a breach in his perspective.[33]

### Ambiguities between Meursault's *moi présent* and his *moi passé*

Just as the last sentences of each chapter in Part 1 of *L'Étranger* mark the end of a day, or the moment at which Meursault conveys his last impressions of the day, the last sentences of each chapter in Part 2 serve also to summarize. They summarize more general periods of time, however, some of which overlap, rather than chronologically terminate a single day or week. These terminal expressions tend toward the lyricism found in Part 1, but become more philosophical and moral as Meursault's imprisonment curtails his senses and thereby broadens and deepens his conscious insight. Usually based on a single metaphor, these résumés concluding each chapter constitute a kind of encomium to the end of each experience portrayed in that chapter. Although they mark moments of Meursault's broadening and deepening awareness, it is far from certain that Meursault alone, given his limitations as presented in the first part of *L'Étranger*, could formulate them. They stand out enough in context to suggest the author's hand in their composition.

As a point of departure for further comparison, the following sentence ends chapter 2 of Part 1 in Meursault's disinterested, factual, flat style typical of his initial point of view:

"J'ai pensé que c'était toujours un dimanche de tiré, que maman était maintenant enterrée, que j'allais reprendre mon travail et que, somme toute, il n'y avait rien de changé." [P. 1140]

In Part 2, however, the last sentence of each chapter epitomizes Meursault's growing awe and certainty of his approaching end in statements as elegiac as they are profound. These statements become generalized and objective enough to stand independent of any narrator, and in this sense resemble Meursault's previously cited maxims from which his *moi présent* is absent. Almost nostalgic in tone, Meursault's personal imprisonment and death take on cosmic proportions as if symbolizing every man's final situation. Chapter 2, for example, ends in the following words:

Le jour finissait et c'était l'heure dont je ne veux pas parler, l'heure sans nom, ou les bruits du soir montaient de tous les étages de la prison dans un cortège de silence. . . . Non, il n'y avait pas d'issue et personne ne peut imaginer ce que sont les soirs dans les prisons.
[P. 1181]

At the close of chapter 3, Meursault formulates his thought in a similarly incongruous way:

Comme si les chemins familiers tracés dans les ciels d'été pouvaient mener aussi bien aux prisons qu'aux sommeils innocents.
[P. 1192]

In such instances, the use of impersonal subjects, the crystallization of preceding events in general statements composed of metaphors, and the addition of a nostalgic, contemplative dimension adhere exclusively neither to Meursault's past narrative nor to his present narration. Although written

primarily in the past tense, the first passage includes the present
as well, and could obtain, too, with regard to the future. The
*moi présent* here adopts a detached attitude so that the attribu-
tion is not clear. Such a perspective is ambiguous, not between the author and his character, but between the *moi
présent* and the *moi passé* of the single point-of-view-subjectivity Meursault.[34]

Included in this same category are the numerous maxims
cited already as generally occurring in the present tense from
which the *moi présent* is completely absent, as well as a great
number of maxims written in the past tense but which, again,
exemplify the same ambiguous perspective. The last chapter of
the book, or Part 3 as it has often been called, displays these
general maxims in abundance.

In the beginning of the last chapter of *L'Étranger*, Meursault is fully present at the narration of his story. He states the
problem of his final moral agony from the first. "Ce qui m'in-
téresse en ce moment c'est s'échapper à la mécanique, de savoir
si l'inévitable peut avoir une issue" (p. 1200). Here Meursault
sets himself a more profound task than could have possibly
been expressed by the same Meursault of Part 1. Initially apparent here, his *moi présent* subsequently becomes technically
defunct in Meursault's frequent generalities which, whether
expressed in the present or in the past tense, belong clearly
neither to Meursault's past narrative nor to his present narration. The following subtle distinction exemplifies Meursault's
longer statements of this nature:

"Car enfin, il y avait une disproportion ridicule entre le judgement
qui l'avait fondée et son déroulement imperturbable à partir du
moment où ce jugement avait été prononcé."          [P. 1201]

The majority of these maxims, however, are short and
memorable in the popular tradition from which they derive,
and they are often stated in the present tense, as in the following series:

"On ne sait jamais ce qui peut arriver."             [P. 1200]

"Mais cela ne parle pas à l'imagination."            [P. 1200]

"On se fait toujours des idées exagérées de ce qu'on ne connaît pas."
[P. 1202]

Besides such general maxims, Meursault expresses at the last his precise personal discoveries more profoundly than would seem credible for a character of his initial limitations. One last sentence stands out as an example of such unexpected profundity on Meursault's part. It encompasses as well as resumes the totality of Meursault's past, present, and future experience in a single statement as lyrical in its expression as it is profound in its significance and yet which conveys precisely the calm certitude of Meursault's final apotheosis:

Du fond de mon avenir, pendant toute cette vie absurde que j'avais menée, un souffle obscur remontait vers moi à travers des années qui n'etaient pas encore venues ce souffle égalisait sur son passage tout ce qu'on me proposait alors dans les années pas plus réelles que je vivais. [P. 1208]

These last profundities not only bear witness to Camus's genius as lyrical artist, but also they reiterate—through Meursault—Camus's positive orientation toward life in all its endeavor which always and ever reasserts its final decision over destruction and death.

In his original discussion of the so-called pictorial novel, as previously noted, Percy Lubbock endorsed the use of the third person as a way of presenting the author's statements in the guise of his character, thus expanding the protagonist's point of view. He did not believe this possible if the story was written in the first person.[35] Camus, however, remains within the confines of the first person throughout *L'Étranger*, yet fulfills Lubbock's definition of the pictorial novel.

Eliminating the intimate personal confession usually associated with first-person narrative partially accounts for Camus's ability to do so. Meursault reports primarily external behavior and external scenes. In addition, Camus's handling of direct and indirect discourse enables him periodically to distance Meursault from the narrating foreground to the narrative background or vice versa, so that he alternately witnesses and par-

ticipates, in the manner envisaged by Lubbock. By endowing
Meursault with such an externally passive and taciturn character, Camus sometimes forces Meursault's *moi présent* to re-
cede and to merge with his narrative background, as in the
instance of the prosecutor already cited. By endowing Meursault with such a strongly lyrical and sensuous orientation to
life, on the other hand, Camus sometimes fills moment-to-
moment descriptions with such sensory detail that Meursault's
*moi passé* seems to focus more sharply and to appear in the
foreground he is describing.

A good example of this latter effect occurs in the last
chapter of *L'Étranger* when Meursault meditates on the possibility of a pardon. The following description is conjectured
in the past tense, but is related in such sensory detail that it
forces itself into the foreground. This description represents
as personal a confession as Meursault ever makes, yet its intimacy of physical detail offers stark contrast to the usual
psychological detail of such confessions. As usual, the physical
detail conveys the psychological effect in *L'Étranger*, yet here
it is expressed in Meursault's own peculiar mode of sensuous
lyricism:

A ce moment, à ce moment seulement, j'avais pour ainsi dire le
droit, je me donnais en quelque sorte la permission d'aborder la
deuxième hypothèse: j'étais gracié. L'ennuyeux, c'est qu'il fallait
rendre moins fougueux cet élan du sang et du corps qui me piquait
les yeux d'une joie insensée. Il fallait que je m'applique à réduire
ce cri, à le raisonner. Il fallait que je sois naturel méme dans cette
hypothèse, pour rendre plus plausible ma résignation dans la première. Quand j'avais réussi, j'avais gagné une heure de calme.
Cela, tout de même, était à considerer.                    [P. 1204]

Meursault's concrete detail, his repetition and restate-
ment of the same motion several times, and his initial "à ce
moment, à ce moment seulement," all add to the impression
that he is experiencing this joy and its subsequent curtailment
as he describes it. His struggle seems to occur at the moment
of its narration, whereas in reality it belongs to his past narrative.

This same confusion between the *moi présent* and the *moi passé* is emphasized by many of Meursault's reiterated expressions. The conditional expression "Je n'aurais pas dû dire cela" occurs most frequently in Part 1 of *L'Étranger*, for example, and disappears in Part 2 as Meursault's hesitations become convictions. The repeated expression "j'avais [or j'ai eu] l'impression que [or de]" is a case in point. Sometimes Camus uses this expression in conjunction with others which indicate a clear-cut difference between the *moi passé* who has participated and the *moi présent* who is narrating:

*"J'avais même l'impression que* cette morte, couchée au milieu d'eux, ne signifiait rien à leurs yeux. Mais *je crois maintenant que* c'était une impression fausse." [P. 1130; italics mine]

The "je crois maintenant" certainly indicates the narrating *moi présent* by contrast to the *moi passé* who was participating, and whose "impression" has subsequently changed. Often, however, Meursault's "impression" is clearly a past one as in the above example, but because of its foresight into present events, it makes the impact of a present without any indicator, such as the "je crois maintenant," to clearly ally it to his *moi présent*. The following examples of this effect include in parentheses the present implications of Meursault's past statements:

"Je me suis expliqué aussi la bizarre *impression que j'avais* (et que *j'ai toujours*) d'être de trop, un peu comme un intrus."
[P. 1183]

*"J'ai eu* un moment (et *j'ai toujours*) *l'impression* ridicule qu'ils étaient là pour me juger." [P. 1130]

*"J'ai eu l'impression (et je l'ai toujours)* que Raymond savait ou il allait, mais c'était sans doute faux." [p. 1163; italics mine]

"Avoir l'impression" is very often accompanied by "bizarre" or "ridicule" or "niaise," which constantly persuades the reader of the contrary. Camus induces the reader to accept Meursault's "impressions" as realities, partially because of Meur-

sault's negation of them, partially because of their foreshadowing, and partially because of the appeal of intuitive impressions
in a nonverbal protagonist like Meursault.

Finally, it is through one of Meursault's bizarre impressions that the ambiguity we have discovered fundamental to
his perspective is best expressed. At only one point in his story
does Meursault clearly extrapolate his point of view from himself long enough to become a spectator of his own actions
through another fictional subjectivity. This occurs during his
trial when Meursault is struck by a young reporter from Paris
who resembles him and who is attentively staring at him.
Meursault briefly comments: "J'ai eu l'impression bizarre
d'être regardé par moi-même" (p. 1184). The young reporter
is looking at Meursault, but Meursault momentarily seems to
be watching himself as well through the reporter's eyes, so that
here Meursault's point of view clearly coincides with that of
the reader who is also watching Meursault.

In addition to the biographical element present here,
derived from Camus's young years as a courtroom reporter,
this scene lends further importance to Meursault's trial and
credence to the most recent interpretations of Meursault's
"strangeness," or alienation. This recent view sees Meursault's
alienation as essentially a linguistic phenomenon which uses
his murder and subsequent trial and condemnation as the
necessary components allowing Meursault's alienation from
himself to be fully explored and relegating Meursault's alienation from society to only secondary consideration. Meursault's
attempts at explaining himself to society at his trial, to the
priest in his cell, and to the reader of his entire story are so
many attempts at capturing and rehabilitating his own identity.
Ultimately, as J.-C. Pariente surmises, "Meursault reste aussi
éloigné de lui-même que les lecteurs puisqu'il ne s'appréhende
que dans son journal: il est bien l'Etranger."[36]

The young reporter witnessing Meursault's trial, therefore,
bodily incorporates both Meursault's distant and estranged
gaze at himself as well as that of the reader and of society. The
reporter might be said to constitute Camus's version of Gide's

*mise en abyme.* It is through close adherence to Meursault's attempts at recapturing this very strangeness and alienation that Camus so skilfully causes the present of his reader to coinside with that of his protagonist. At the moment his narrating *moi présent* temporarily identifies with the young reporter, Meursault's essential ambiguity literally stares him in the face. Otherwise, it remains unresolved until the last line of the last page of the end of his story.

## CHAPTER 4

*Dans la measure où il est esthétiquement réussi, chaque roman pose un monde.*

—Robert Champigny

*Ts'ui Pên must have said once: "I am withdrawing to write a book." And another time: "I am withdrawing to construct a labyrinth." Everyone imagined two works; to no one did it occur that the book and the labyrinth were one and the same thing.*

—Jorge Luis Borges

*Things fall apart; the centre cannot hold;*

\*       \*       \*

*Surely some revelation is at hand . . .*
—W. B. Yeats

# THE LABYRINTH AS ARCHETYPAL IMAGE OF THE NEW NOVEL

With Alain Robbe-Grillet, fictional perspective takes the final step prepared for by Sartre and Camus of subordinating the entire spatio-temporal field to its *trompe-l'oeil* aspects. Robbe-Grillet's fictional world presents a single microcosmic enigma, a labyrinth in which as many readers are led astray as successfully enter and find an exit. In *Dans le Labyrinthe* Robbe-Grillet introduces and constantly maintains an ambiguous, enigmatic double perspective with unabashed temerity. It is from the labyrinth of its title that this slim volume comes to represent the vision not only of its author, but of the entire group of New Novelists and their disciples who continue to proliferate in France.

Creating a fiction about the creation of a fiction, Robbe-Grillet in *Dans le Labyrinthe* succeeds more completely than either Sartre or Camus, or indeed than any other New Novelist, in eliminating his personal voice from the novel. Robbe-Grillet's first-person narrator begins and ends the *Labyrinthe* by narrating a story about a soldier, whose third-person perspective determine his story within the story. Although Robbe-Grillet succeeds through this double perspective in eliminating his personal voice from the novel, he does not even attempt to eliminate the narrator's voice from intervening in his narrative so that interventions by the narrator will occur in the place of the more usual interventions by the author.[1] Although such a technique seems simply to replace the author by the narrator, in fact, the author of *Dans le Labyrinthe* controls the fictional domain of the narrator, who in turn controls the fictional domain of the soldier. Robbe-Grillet's peculiar method of depicting an independent narrator in the throes of the creative process at the very outset of the *Labyrinthe* effectively adheres to Sartre's avowed esthetic purpose of setting both author and reader equidistant from the narrator who creates his fiction independent of either, yet dependent to a certain extent on both.

Rather than allow his narrator to discuss the creative process within his own fictional domain, as Proust, Gide, and Joyce have done, Robbe-Grillet introduces a narrator who shows the creative process at work in the construction of a fictional world different from his own, albeit one which is a reflection of his own. Robbe-Grillet's narrator does not reign as protagonist of the fictional field he creates; indeed, whether he is present within his narrative at all has been questioned.[2]

It is Robbe-Grillet's development of reflection as a literary technique which determines the import of his novel. Although consciousness can proceed from author to narrator to character with no reversal in this novel, forms—objects, itineraries, events and persons within their physical limitations—can reflect precisely as in a mirror image, or approximately as in a shadow, from the narrative domain to the narrator's domain, and from both fictional domains to life itself. Gérard Genette has rightly termed Robbe-Grillet's predilection for this technique of reflection the "soul" of his work, and one which constantly postulates its double nature as dependent upon its sameness or its otherness every time a form, an image, or an event recurs.[3]

The game of Chinese boxes is often evoked as best expressing Robbe-Grillet's technique of repetition with variations of single scenes. A series of different, flat, plastic, geometric shapes of various hues placed one on top of the other in such a way that their overlapping center color remains constant while their edges vary in combinations of both shapes and colors might render a more exact image of Robbe-Grillet's technique. Each form, scene, or event in a novel by Robbe-Grillet repeats itself in various reflections which always vary so that ultimately each retains a constant core of sameness with slight variations. Robbe-Grillet's emphasis is upon the reiteration of single forms under various guises within a specific fictional world, so that his work lends itself easily to mythical and archetypal interpretation. Emphasis upon sameness and reflection works toward the unity of the work, the unity of the point of view, and the unity of the fictional world which itself is double in *Dans le Labyrinthe*.

Chronology in this novel initially seems to dissolve, though a spare succession of events does become evident upon rereading. Two spatial areas, however, are clearly defined: the room and the city. Certain events occur only in the room, others, only in the city; however, a small number of them occur both in the room and in the city. Also, past events impose themselves on the narrative by psychological association, or by visual association, where they are relived in the present rather than remembered in the past.

Robbe-Grillet's concern with method, with the functioning of the feverish or creative consciousness, overrides his concern with its end result. The feverish consciousness in *Dans le Labyrinthe* is equated with the creative act within specified limits. These limits are imposed by objects, which carry the creative imagination in its effort to relate all elements into a unity or at least into a reflective relationship.[4] Spatial juxtapositions determine progression, and reiteration of the same spaces, objects, and configurations determines the rhythm of the narrative.

Although critics have maintained that Robbe-Grillet willfully confuses the spatio-temporal framework in *Dans le Labyrinthe* in order to create a dream state, it seems more relevant to say that the work resembles a daydream or a fantasy. The narrator imagines the soldier's narrative, but he fancies that the soldier arbitrarily links his experience in sequences which occur to him in seeming misalliance. Every element in the sequence of the soldier's story, in fact, has some basis in his conscious experience, so that, like the day residue in dreams, elements return in apparently arbitrary sequence as reruns of real events that have occurred in the soldier's life. The progression of these scenes depends more upon the soldier's present condition, which is sometimes feverish and continually fatigued, than upon a clear chronological presentation. By careful rereading, only a weak chronology emerges to help put the story in some orderly sequence: the story progresses from the street, to the young woman's apartment, to the barracks, to the café, back to the street where he is shot, and finally to the original apartment where he dies. The entire story takes place in one day, one night, and the following day.[5]

As disconcerting as his quixotic temporal sequence, however, is Robbe-Grillet's spatial juxtaposition in *Dans le Labyrinthe*. Moving events outside the narrator's room reflecting stable elements within his room, the picture furnishing both décor and point-of-view-subjectivities for the narrative, and the soldier obsessively reiterating the same scenes and events with only slight variations, disconcert quite as much as the eternal present in which the narrative unfolds. Furthermore, the room in which the soldier dies reflecting point by point the room of the narrator is even more disturbing as the story impinges upon the narrator's world, and as both fictions in turn impinge upon the real world of the reader. Hence, most critics were initially preoccupied by the double nature of objects such as the lamp–lamppost, bedroom slippers–army boots, dust–snow, picture–café. Other analogues, although somewhat more obscure, are: the slow but steady itinerary of the fly and its disappearance in the red curtains–the soldier's wanderings and ultimate death; the bayonet in the room–the bayonet in the soldier's box; the many resemblances between the sick soldier and his dead comrade searching for a lost father–the boy's soldier-father who perhaps deserted, but at least was similarly defeated at Reichenfels. At one point, the soldier places his feet

exactly in each footprint made by the boy, and suddenly thinks
he has seen himself pass this way before; there are many suggestions that the boy and the soldier are one and the same,
both left by a father, or at least that the soldier serves as a
substitute father for the boy. Through this kind of analogous
duplication, Robbe-Grillet not only exaggerates artifice and
disconcerts the reader, but also, and more importantly, asserts
the duplication of his phenomenal world "in the labyrinth."

Dreams, daydreams, and thought being in themselves
phenomena with a double aspect, Robbe-Grillet's peculiarly
physical affirmation of the existence of things, events, and
gestures counter-balances the dreamlike metaphysical aspect
in this work. Just as these are double phenomena, the point of
view in this novel is double; it is a fictional world composed
of two domains or sites, each of which corresponds to one of
the two perspectives.


## Manipulation of person


Robbe-Grillet lends to each of the domains of his fictional
world, the city and the room, a different subjectivity: the
soldier and the narrator. But it is the two domains which
primarily concern Robbe-Grillet rather than the point-of-view-
subjectives whose perspectives reveal each of them. His
stylistic emphasis upon description, moreover, nearly eliminates perspective by its use of inanimate objects as subjects of
sentences and by its many passives and verbal participles
which create an impersonal atmosphere. His style objectifies
and generalizes, but to label *Dans le Labyrinthe* an objective
novel without personal reference is patently to misunderstand
its esthetic. It is often impersonal, but never nonpersonal. The
personal vision of the narrator or of the soldier informs the
novel at every instant so that descriptive passages belong to
one or to the other domain, and often seem to belong ambiguously to both.[6]

To facilitate and to emphasize the dual aspect of his fictional world, Robbe-Grillet has resorted to two perspectives, but the third-person perspective of the soldier is formally contained within that of the narrator, so that the analogies common to both belong to a single world. Ambiguity is implicit within this method of emphasis upon similarity, with differences melted into a "rumination d'images,"[7] which are mostly visual, but sometimes auditory. Perception and imagination are not clearly distinguished, so that the narrator remains in a fog of undifferentiated sight and fantasy throughout the book, and the soldier from the beginning seems to be chronically fatigued, feverish, and dying. The similarity of the soldier's and the narrator's styles of expression risks flattening *Dans le Labyrinthe* into a monologue. The differences are initially established, however, by assigning each domain to a different *porteur de perspective.*

The initial point of view is established in the first sentence: "Je suis seul, ici, maintenant, bien à l'abri" (p. 9).[8] Although this sentence solidly stabilizes the narrator within the interior of his room, such a statement does not suffice from a literary standpoint firmly to anchor perspective within the fictional field of the novel. It merely describes the state of being of the first-person narrator, a protected, passive state. The narrator is not integrated by any action, comment, or judgment into his fictional field; there are no tactile or kinetic notations to anchor him firmly within his surroundings.

"Je," "ici," and "maintenant," being always true, or pertaining invariably to anyone at the present moment, posit the atemporal domain of a narrator eternally present but not situated in relation to what is narrated. This first sentence announces already the emphatic spatial orientation of the novel, the stasis of the narrator and of his domain, the room, as well as of his behavior, which consists of imagining, rather than of the kinetic participation which belongs to the domain of the soldier.

In addition, the description following this first sentence is attributed to wholly impersonal subjects: "On," "il y a," "le vent," "la poussière," "la pluie," which, along with passive verb forms, tend to objectify and to generalize perspective. Following the first sentence, the narrator seems to disappear from the fictional field almost entirely.

After the narrator initially situates himself in the first sentence of the book, he does not speak of himself in the first person again until the end, where he reveals he is a doctor who has tried in vain to save the sick soldier. The clear vision of the doctor-narrator's descriptive dénouement at the last offers striking contrast to the final blurred and limited vision of the feverish, dying soldier. During his final agonizing moments, the soldier's vision becomes progressively hazy and illogical. After the soldier's death, the narrator logically and rationally resolves the principal elements of the narrative. This is the only passage in the book in which the narrator's expression so clearly differs from the soldier's and, in fact, from his own earlier style, that it tends to grant a separate point of view to the doctor. On the very last pages of the *Labyrinthe,* however, and throughout the text until immediately after the soldier's death, no stylistic change differentiates the soldier's perspective from the narrator's, so that the reader is made to think his way through the ambiguous labyrinthine perspectives.

The first thirty pages which follow the initial sentence of *Dans le Labyrinthe* constitute an exposition of the text best interpreted as the interior monologue of the narrator in search of his narrative. Such a strangely impersonal interior monologue consisting of pure description without personal reference to the narrator disconcerts and seemingly eliminates him altogether from the fictional field. Yet, this narrator cannot be totally eliminated after his first statement solidly situating himself in the spatio-temporal here and now. He initially places himself in the room by contrast to what is outside the room, and his descriptive style remains consistent throughout so that no other character intervenes, nor does the author impose another perspective until the soldier materializes.

The second sentence of the *Labyrinthe* begins: "Dehors il pleut . . . ," the third: "Dehors il y a du soleil . . . ," and the fourth sentence returns to: "Ici le soleil n'entre pas . . ." (p. 9). "Dehors and "ici" refer to the two separate domains, which are introduced immediately by reference to the narrator's placement, so that they both initially derive from his single perspective. Whenever "dehors" and "ici" are repeated within the novel, they relate both domains to the narrator's single, and therefore unifying, point of view. This occurs notably at the very end of the novel after the soldier's death where "dehors" and "ici" again reaffirm the single narrator's perspective eternally embracing two domains.[9]

By a continual switching of locale, from the stable, immutable and silent interior with its concrete surfaces, forms, and textures to the mutable, shifting, animated exterior with its continual snowstorm, Robbe-Grillet initially centers perspective within the narrator located in his room, who imagines the world of the city outside his room.

The narrator describes the room as it is perceived, and constructs the narrative city as it is projected or imagined from the given elements of his room much as Mallarmé does in his sonnet in *yx*. No typographical or verbal indication separates the two domains, however, designating one as real and the other as fabricated, so that one seems to equal the other. They are equally vital and equally present, that is, but they are not equally solid. The room is described at length with its solid, stable, and immovable objects, while the city takes form gradually as a windy rainstorm, a scintillating heatwave, or a whirling snowstorm containing elements drawn primarily as reflections or analogues of the objects and furnishings within the room. The city is obviously derived from the room, just as later the soldier and the boy, as well as most of the minor subjectivities, will be derived from the picture within the room. Here, again, is Gide's *mise en abyme*, or the "fiction within the fiction," indicating that this New Novel joins all others in reflecting upon itself as symptomatically predicated by Sartre in his preface to *Portrait d'un inconnu*.[10]

The room, finally, makes a more solid impact than does the city, which evidences only an ephemeral temporality. In this way Robbe-Grillet initially emphasizes the domain of the narrator, the creator, the one who imagines as more fundamental or peculiarly "real" than the ephemeral domain of the fantasy the daydream, the created fiction. He first establishes his narrator in a kind of Platonic cave which merely reflects the different and separate "reality" outside. But soon the fiction of the soldier's narrative usurps and eclipses the narrator's domain almost entirely. There is no syntactical transition between the narrator's external surroundings and his internal narrative. What he perceives in his room and what he imagines in his narrative remain subsequently undifferentiated. Sometimes a change of tense indicates this shift from perception to imagination, but not consistently, thus adding further enigma to Robbe-Grillet's labyrinth.

The first-person narrator all but vanishes in this exposition consisting mostly of objective description which is couched in geometrical terms and which notes mainly external forms and shapes, markings and paths. It is only by direct reference to place that the reader understands whether he is in the perceived reality of the narrator's room or in the imagined fiction of his city.

In this respect, perspective is purely visual, equated with a camera which focuses alternately upon interior narrative and exterior surroundings. Transitions from one domain to the other are made by way of "dehors" and "ici," or by objects which reflect their analogues. The sound of boots on the pavement, for example, is reflected from the silence of the felt slippers in the room (p. 12); a seemingly exterior "wall" becomes the wall of the room (p. 15); the "fil incandescent" of the lamp on the table reflects the "filament" of the streetlight (p. 16); the path in the snow is reflected from the path on the dust-covered floor of the room (p. 18); the slow, steady progress of the fly in the room reflects the similar itinerary of the soldier (p. 20); and finally the mysterious box present in the

room is physically projected, rather than reflected by an analogue, into the narrative (p. 22).

Other changes of place and of focus are affected by
following the direction in which a character is looking, again
equating perspective with a camera, as the following examples
demonstrate:

"C'est pas mon père," dit l'enfant.
Et il *tourne la tête* vers le rectangle noir de la porte vitrée.
Dehors il neige. . . .
                                                    [P. 31; italics mine]

*Ses yeux ont quitté* le soldat pour se porter vers le bout de la
rue. . . . Et il *ramène les yeux* vers ce soldat malvêtu. . . .
                                                    [P. 35; italics mine]

Son *regard ayant rencontré celui du soldat,* elle demande:
"Qu'est-ce que c'est?"
                                                    [P. 56; italics mine]

*Les yeux du patron ont quitté la tête* blême du soldat qui se
détache toujours sur le fond noir de la nuit, . . . pour livrer
bientôt passage à l'enfant.
                                                    [P. 39; italics mine]

Making external descriptions without commentary or
observation of a personal nature reduces the narrator to an
observer; he does not interpret. Point of view becomes a center
of perception limited to vision rather than of conscious interpretation or of a personal *prise de conscience.*[11] Consciousness
consists in the power of observation in *Dans le Labyrinthe,* so
that the feverish vision of the soldier limited by the snowstorm
or blinded by the sudden chiaroscuro in the corridors and in
the rooms of the barracks determines point of view rather than
any mental process. The soldier's vision blurs continuously:
the boy backs away or disappears in one, two, or three glimpses
beneath the lamplight; the barracks' corporal retreats step by
step from vision; characters continually withdraw or leave or
go away from the soldier. The narrator's vision, on the contrary, becomes ever more clear and complete. He first notes
only forms, then fills in more detail, adds movement, then

color, and finally completes entire scenes which relate the last wanderings and death of an unknown soldier.[12]

Dependence upon vision emphasizes first the décor of the city against which the characters come to life like marionettes on a stage. The narrative consists, in fact, of lengthy descriptions of the décor against which miniature dramas are enacted. These descriptions, often in the past tense, distance the reader from the fictional scene, causing the ensuing dialogue in the present to stand out more vividly.

The first, and typical, example of a miniature drama coming to life against a décor which has been described at length takes place when the picture first materializes. Following the lengthy description of the picture are two paragraphs of transition, in which the décor seems to have taken on life though the figure of the soldier does not yet move. For the short space of these two transitional paragraphs, the narrator's vision reads into the painted décor the life he imagines it to acquire. Up to this point he has described the painting in the present tense, moving from one group to another until his gaze fixes upon three soldiers seated at a table. Of the three, he singles out one, and then suddenly begins describing the décor surrounding this soldier in the *passé composé*. At once the glass of wine has been drunk, the café has been vacated, the light has lowered, and finally the child, now standing, begins to speak. The dialogue between the soldier and the child constitutes the first small drama which begins the narrative.

The two brief paragraphs mentioned above which serve as a transition from the frozen picture to the first line of the dialogue are quoted below in order to demonstrate how the narrative begins to formulate from the narrator's point of view. There is no indication besides the change of tense that perspective has moved from the narrator's external perception of the picture to an internal animation of his imagination; the imagined narrative remains on the same plane as the perceived picture.

L'homme est assis, raide, les mains posées à plat sur la table que recouvre une toile cirée à carreaux blancs et rouges.

Il a fini son verre depuis longtemps. Il n'a pas l'air de songer à s'en aller. Pourtant, autour de lui, le café s'est vidé de ses derniers clients. La lumière a baissé, le patron ayant éteint la plus grande partie des lampes avant de quitter lui-même la salle. Le soldat, les yeux grands ouverts, continue de fixer la pénombre devant soi, à quelques mètres devant soi, là où se dresse l'enfant, immobile et rigide lui aussi, debout, les bras le long du corps. Mais c'est comme si le soldat ne voyait pas l'enfant— ni l'enfant ni rien d'autre. Il a l'air de s'être endormi de fatigue, assis contre la table, les yeux grands ouverts.

C'est l'enfant qui prononce les premières paroles. Il dit: "Tu dors?"                                                         [Pp. 29–30]

All descriptions of the soldier up to this point have been of his unmoving stance and grayish color, making of him little more than a statue, a part of the snow-filled décor; otherwise, he has been described as a painted figure staring amidst the equally fixed, painted crowd in the café. Just after his initial dialogue with the boy which begins with the child's query quoted above, however, he is described walking through the snow-filled street, thereby fully anchoring himself within his fictional field: "Arrivé à un croisement, le soldat hésite, cherche du regard les plaques qui devraient indiquer le nom de cette voie transversale" (p. 31). Later the soldier is further anchored solidly by the boy's detailed description of him (pp. 33–34).

Just at this point when he first speaks to the child, the soldier's perspective takes over the narrative until his death, interrupted periodically by the return of the narrator's focus to his room and to the picture. After the soldier's death, the narrator reveals he is the doctor, not by statement as does Camus's Rieux in La Peste, but by anchoring himself more firmly in the fictional field of the novel at the last. Until that time he remains an observer and dreamer who interrupts the narrative periodically, but who seems neither completely integrated into it nor completely eliminated from it until he finally integrates himself more fully at the last.

Just after his first dialogue then, the dominant central perspective is that of the soldier, though it is interrupted sporadically by the narrator. Each time a description of the room or of the picture, the "Defeat of Reichenfels," appears, the narrative has returned to the narrator's perspective. Otherwise, the soldier's perspective determines the action. "L'homme s'est arrêté. Sans bouger le reste du corps, il a tourné la tête en arrière" (p. 34). This purely external description belongs to the soldier's perspective, but could be made as well by the narrator or by another fictional character observing the soldier. There are many such descriptive passages in which perspective is ambiguous at best. Only rarely are they interspersed with commentaries which can be attributed to one single perspective. A statement such as the following, for instance, can only be attributed to the soldier who makes it, since it is not observable to the reader or to any other fictional character present in the scene, such as the boy in this instance: "Mais la question qu'il allait poser n'est pas la bonne" (p. 34). Such expressions are rare, however, and are often written in the past tense, as if personal thoughts normally express themselves in the past, or perhaps in order to differentiate such comment of an internal, personal nature from the external objective description. Memory seems somehow allied with such past-tense expressions, especially with the imperfect tense.

The initial exposition of *Dans le Labyrinthe* reveals the author's techniques of composition in germ, as it were. Indeed, the repetition of the same scene under different weather conditions, the several tenses following each other, and the frequency of choices, repetitions, questions, and negations do seem to reveal various possible developments of the narrative which present themselves to the narrator as he is deciding upon his preferred mode of expression.[13] Because his beginning interior monologue is purely descriptive, however, he becomes hypothetical, an observer and a dreamer rather than a narrator. He neither concludes nor judges, though he sometimes comments. Rather than directly attributable to him, his comments appear mainly in the form of parentheses, questions, negations, and choices in the tentative, hesitant trials and errors of his creative imagination. These same comments are sometimes attributable to the soldier, however, and very often to either the soldier or to the narrator. Their similar modes of expression inextricably ally the two perspectives without possibility of separation. Through his particular use of indirect discourse in *L'Étranger*, Camus sporadically allowed the merging of Meursault's perspective with that of his interlocutors. Taking one step further, through his particular use of description in the *Labyrinthe*, Robbe-Grillet inextricably merges the two perspectives of narrator and soldier for the greater part of the entire novel. Furthermore, these numerous parenthetical remarks, questions, negations, and choices constitute the primary technique by which Robbe-Grillet fosters and maintains the Sartrean *trompe-l'oeil* ambiguities and enigmas which twist and contort his text into its sinuous labyrinthine structure. The following serve as examples of this aspect of Robbe-Grillet's technique.

Questions and parenthetical remarks written in the text between parentheses or hyphens are the most common form of abrupt intervention in the predominantly descriptive narrative of the novel. Sometimes clearly made by the narrator, in the first thirty pages, for example, and sometimes clearly made by the soldier during the ensuing narrative, the great majority of these passages remain ambiguous. They can be attributed either to the narrator's hesitant search for the precise word which might best further his narrative, or to the soldier's search for lucidity and direction in the strange city, wandering through the blinding snow, and burdened by fatigue and fever.

Descriptive detail between parentheses added to the text is the least disconcerting of the narrator's interventions because it extends the objective description of the text without an enigmatic jolt such as that afforded by questions and by series of alternate choices. Although such detailed precisions extend the general descriptive text, they represent personal comment or internal incursions into the text by the narrator or by the soldier. The detail and the precision of such descriptive additions often seem superfluous at best, but they do

slightly twist and contort Robbe-Grillet's syntax in the labyrinthine manner achieved more successfully by other, stronger
parenthetical comments. Such descriptive detail present at the
beginning and at the end of the book or during passages which
take place in the room can be attributed unequivocally to the
narrator; in the longer text of the narrative, they can clearly
be attributed to the soldier. The following examples typify
such parenthetical comments which detail precisely:

—car il n'y a pas un souffle d'air—                    [P. 15]

(un angle droit augmenté de la moitié d'un angle droit)     [P. 21]

(rendus même plus nets par leur bordure verticale restée noire)
                                                       [P. 23]

—d'essayer, plutôt, car le passage est malaisé—        [P. 27]

(c'est-à-dire vers les portemanteaux)                  [P. 27]

(bien qu'aucune différence ne soit sensible à l'oeil)  [P. 76]

—moins vite, même, du fait qu'il y est placé sur le bord—
                                                      [P. 179]

(mais les insignes absents de sa vareuse étaient ceux de caporal,
dont la trace restait nettement visible sur l'étoffe brune)
                                                      [P. 187]

Sur la tablette repose un objet assez long, pas très élevé—un
centimètre ou deux, seulement, du côté le plus haut—qui ne
peut être identifié, sous cet angle de vue, n'étant pas placé
suffisamment au bord du marbre (il est même possible qu'il
s'étende, en largeur, bien plus qu'il ne paraît). . . .     [P. 191]

More disconcerting than descriptive detail, alternate
choices for the further development of the narrative, especially in the opening pages of the book, indicate uncertainty and
hesitation on the part of the narrator. On the first page the
choice between "Dehors il pleut . . . , dehors il fait froid
. . . , dehors il y a du soleil" (p. 9), narrows to "Dehors il
neige" (p. 11) and finally submits even this possibility to a
choice of tenses several pages later: "Dehors il neige. Dehors
il a neigé, il neigeait, dehors il neige" (p. 14). Other such
initial choices are:

La seule poussière provient de la chambre elle-même: des raies
du plancher peut-être, ou bien du lit, ou des rideaux, ou des
cendres dans la cheminée.                                          [P. 10]

l'emplacement occupé pendant quelque temps—pendant quelques
heures, quelques jours, minutes, semaines—par de menus objets
                                                                  [P. 10]

On dirait une fleur. . . . Ou bien ce serait une figurine vaguement
humaine. . . . Ce pourrait être aussi un poignard.              [P. 13]

Sentences in the conditional mood and those including
such expressions as "peut-être" or "sans doute" add to the
uncertainty and hesitation either of the narrator during his
composing or of the soldier during his wandering. They again
represent incursions of the internal thought of the narrator
or of the soldier into the normally external description of the
text. Such expressions disconcert by suddenly introducing into
otherwise factual passages doubt about their veracity. It is
only by relating such interjections to the narrator's creative
method by trial and elimination, or to the soldier's alien and
unaccustomed exposure to a strange place, that we see them as
adding to the text at all. In every case in which choices, verbs
in the conditional tense, or passages containing "peut-être"
and the like appear during the narrative section of the novel,
which is dominated by the soldier's point of view, they suggest
intervention by the narrator's indecisive creative imagination.
These passages are ambiguous, therefore, lending themselves
equally well to either the soldier's or to the narrator's perspective. In the following examples, only the first one seems
to belong clearly to the narrator; the others remain ambiguous.

les molletières . . . à moins qu'il ne s'agisse ici de leggins, ou
même de bottes . . .                                            [P. 90]

Si le dernier personnage n'était pas sorti par la même porte . . .
il aurait fait entrer le jour. . . .                            [P. 61]

peut-être le mari de la jeune femme . . . et peut-être le père
de l'enfant                                                     [P. 66]

—qui porterait aussi bien, d' ailleurs, des chaussures aux semelles
identiques (les mêmes chaussures, peut-être, venant du même
magasin). . . .                                                 [P. 77]

—la jeune femme, sans doute, ou quelque camarade de régiment—
[P. 67]

Il faudrait donc se pencher en avant, soulever le pan de toile cirée et jeter un coup d'oeil sous la table, entre les quatre pieds carrés qui s'amincissent vers le bas—ou bien, s'amincissant vers le bas, mais en bois tourné, cannelés, devenant à l'extrémité supérieure cylindriques et lisses, s'achevant au sommet en quatre cubes portant une rose sculptée sur deux de leurs faces—ou bien . . . le soldat regarde encore le portrait sur le mur de fond. . . .
[P. 89]

As ambiguous and as uncertain as "peut-être" and as the conditional tense, the verb "devoir" appears frequently in the *Labyrinthe*. Used most often in the past form "a dû," this verb continually renders the text in which it appears uncertain. If it belongs to the narrator's point of view, as frequently seems to be the case, then the narrator is often undecided about the actions of his characters. If it belongs to the soldier, then he displays a lack of knowledge about his own actions too extreme to remain plausible. If it belongs to the author, then he is as undecided vis-à-vis his characters as the narrator seems to be. The author clearly means to unsettle his fictional field, rendering it more nearly labyrinthine with such loose ends and unsolved enigmas. In the following examples, only the last one might clearly indicate the soldier's perspective, in which case this incident would represent the only one he wholly imagines. All the rest directly describe his experience, which is often slightly distorted by his fever. (All italics are mine.)

Le soldat *a donc dû* le rencontrer plusieurs fois. . . .     [P. 35]

C'était peut-être à ce carrefour-ci que la rencontre *devait* avoir lieu.     [P. 52]

Comme la fenêtre est située au dernier étage, tous ces ronds de lumière *doivent* apparaître lointains et pâles. . . .     [P. 78]

(Le courant d'air *a dû*, pourtant, entrainer la lampe dans le sens longitudinal, mais le plan des oscillations a tourné peu à peu, sans que leur amplitude diminue de façon sensible, et l'ombre raccourcie de l'homme apparaît et disparaît, tantôt à droite, tantôt à gauche, alternativement.)     [P. 99]

L'impression *a dû* lui traverser l'esprit (mais cela lui paraît à présent incroyable) que l'homme après lequel il courait depuis son arrivée dans la ville était justement, *peut-être,* celui-là, avec son parapluie au fourreau de soie, son manteau fourré, sa grosse bague.                                                                 [P. 152]

Le soldat *a dû* finir par se taire, car ils sont à présent de nouveau muets l'un en face de l'autre, figés dans la même position qu'au début. . . .                                                                [P. 153]

L'occasion le plus vraisemblable serait donc un congé exceptionnel de quelques heures. . . . Aucun camarade de régiment ne l'accompagnait, car la jeune femme *figureait* alors sur le cliché, à côté du soldat; c'est elle qui *a dû* prendre la photo, avec son propre appareil; elle a même *sans doute* consacré tout un rouleau de pellicules à l'événement, et elle a ensuite fait agrandir le meilleure.
                                                                          [P. 68]

Equally ambiguous, but even more enigmatic, are the numerous questions sporadically interjected throughout the text. Like parenthetical comments, questions in the *Labyrinthe* indicate the intrusion of internal indecision, again seemingly attributed to the soldier, but equally valid if attributed to the narrator assailed by doubts about his narrative. Further complicating the ambiguous source of these questions is the strong suspicion that basically they might very well be posed for the reader by the author. These questions remain unanswered in the text and thus convey gratuitous doubt, not to say an unhealthy obsession with detail. The following quotations exemplify such enigmatic questions:

La porte vient-elle de s'ouvrir pour laisser le passage à un nouvel arrivant, qui étonnerait le gamin par son costume insolite: un soldat, par exemple?                                                    [P. 49]

une porte . . . Ou bien était-elle déjà ouverte tout à l'heure?
                                                                          [P. 56]

sa mère (est-ce sa mère?) vient d'introduire. . . .          [P. 65]

une chaise qui est située (vient-elle de l'y mettre?) devant . . .
                                                                          [P. 70]

La femme a donc fini par céder? . . . Cette scène se serait-elle déroulée hors de sa présence? Mais où et quand?          [P. 91]

(N'y avait-il pas de bouton au rez-de-chaussée, puisque la montée
s'est effectuée dans le noir?)                          [P. 101]

Only in rare instances does Robbe-Grillet clearly indicate
the source of such questions. The following passage, for example, attributes an internal question to the soldier in traditional fictional form:

Le soldat se propose de le demander à la jeune femme. Le sait-
elle, seulement, dans cette chambre sans fenêtre?        [P. 196]

Interventions due uniquely to the soldier's internal
thought appear only rarely by comparison with those ambiguous questions and comments which obtain for both
soldier and narrator. Flashbacks sometimes include normal
transitions which indicate a shift from his external perception
to his internal recall, as in one short paragraph beginning: "Le
soldat ferme les yeux, et retrouve les flocons blancs qui
descendent avec lenteur . . ." (pp. 58–59). More often, however, the soldier's external perception shifts to an internal recall without transition. In these instances, his flashbacks consist of former visual perceptions reiterated out of their original
context rather than of any internal comment, thought, or
judgment on his part. The soldier's uncommonly acute sensitivity to minute details of his surroundings and his obsessive
mental reenactments of former events, including verbatim
repetitions of dialogues,[14] interspersed as they are by negatives, suggest his desperate struggle for lucidity of the moment, his grasping for life by rejecting other scenes and places
which impose themselves from within his internal memory.
The following paragraph exemplifies a flashback to the
soldier's internal imagination without the usual transitional
warning; the regular rhythm of light and dark in the corridor
where he is standing seems to mesmerize the soldier into a fantasy repetition of what has previously occurred. Since his
cognition of the light and the corridor is visual, as is his recall
of the snow scene with the boy, perception and imagination
are indistinguishable, and so the entire scene deceptively
occurs on a single plane.

Noir. Déclic. Clarté jaune. Déclic. Noir. Déclic. Clarté grise.
Déclic. Noir. Et les pas qui résonnent sur le plancher du couloir.
Et les pas qui résonnent sur l'asphalte, dans rue figée par le
gel. Et la neige qui commence à tomber. Et la silhouette inter-
mittente de gamin qui s'amenuise, là-bas, de lampadaire en
lampadaire.                                                        [P. 61]

Negatives abound within the soldier's point of view
throughout, but they tend to proliferate as he nears death (cf.
pp. 182, 193–95). The negative is used ambiguously, however, when the word "non" is periodically interjected into
several important passages (cf. pp. 95, 96, 97, 160, 193).
One critic believes that such interjections must be attributed
to the narrator, who first hesitates in the development of his
narrative, then negates the preceding passage by his emphatic
"non," and finally continues his narrative from a different
point of departure.[15] He cites the following passage as the
prime example of this technique.

Il (le soldat) remarque à cet instant que la porte est entrouverte:
porte, couloir, porte, vestibule, porte, puis enfin une pièce
éclairée, et une table avec un verre vide. . . . Non. Porte
entrebâillée. Couloir. Escalier. Femme qui monte en courant
d'étage en étage, tout au long de l'étroit colimaçon où son
tablier gris tournoie en spirale. . . . Non. Au-dessus de la commode
une gravure encadrée de bois noir est fixée. . . . Non. Non. Non.
                                                                  [P. 96]

Judging from the style in this passage as compared to
other passages containing similar negative protestations, it
would seem equally plausible to attribute these interjections to
the soldier, who again makes the effort to reject his fantasy-
repetitions in order to restore his lucidity and to return to his
present milieu. If these several instances of "non" do indicate
interventions of the narrator, then it must follow that the
narrator interrupts his narrative even more frequently than has
been already suggested, and with even less warning, so that
his presence or absence as commentator within the narrative
becomes totally arbitrary and obscure.

But what is the importance of these enigmatic incursions
into the text by the narrator? What is the result of Robbe-

Grillet's establishing such clear ambiguities in both perspectives of *Dans le Labyrinthe*? We have seen that the narrator is just a *metteur en scène* initially, who prepares the visual objects for his spectator. This is particularly evident in the first thirty pages designated here as the exposition of the novel. After that, the narrator becomes a commentator and judge within the narrative, but his interventions are not specifically attributed to him, and so the atmosphere of uncertainty, or query, and of unresolved enigmas leads either to distrust and eventual rejection or to an active arousal of the reader's intellectual and critical acumen. Everything stated may or may not be true. Robbe-Grillet grasps or implicates the reader in this way so that he interprets on his own, accepts or rejects possibilities offered, and thus inadvertently becomes a part of the fictional world. The reader is forced at least to interpret independently, if not to create practically out of whole cloth, the story along with Robbe-Grillet's narrator. Most critics of Robbe-Grillet, whether sympathetic or otherwise, have sensed in various ways his avowed intention of inflicting his fictional world upon his reader, of forcing his reader's identification with and participation in his fictional world, or of arousing his reader's lucid sense of intellectual challenge through the *données* of his fictional world.[16] Those critics who have understood the phenomenological bent of Robbe-Grillet's literary expression have interpreted him most clearly and with the greatest insight on this point, as, for example, John Sturrock, when he writes: "The methods of the New Novel will remain mysterious and apparently perverse unless this crucial distinction is kept in view: that the mind is free but the eye is not."[17]

## Manipulation of time

*Dans le Labyrinthe* occurs predominantly in an eternal present tense. Robbe-Grillet's use of the *passé composé,* in particular, more nearly fits Sartre's definition of that tense as a "succession

de présents inertes" than does Camus's use of it in
*L'Étranger*.[18] Robbe-Grillet's frequent use of past participles
as modifiers, of present participles, and of the passive voice,
moreover, allows the present mood to prevail in *Dans le Labyrinthe.* But the question of chronology in this novel has remained confused and generally misinterpreted. A prosaic,
progressive narrative thread develops in spite of dead ends,
wrong turns, false starts, and blind alleys. Perception and
memory and thought are often confused, but not chronically
or continuously; they have a logic of their own specific to this
work.

Remembered impressions are most often noted in the imperfect, whereas remembered action is noted in the *passé
composé.* Both past tenses are used in conjunction with the
present for dramatic effect rather than to indicate temporality.[19] The narrative consists largely of description interspersed with infrequent scenes of dialogue between the soldier
and one other character. Often the present-tense dialogue is
framed by past-tense description. It is safe to assume that the
entire event has occurred previously when it is narrated in the
past tense, but that part of it—the dialogue—is relived verbatim, and is therefore transcribed in the present tense. The
present-tense dialogue enclosed by past description is merely
a verbatim report of the soldier's memory made more striking
by its contrast with its past context. This requires a shift in
the reader's mind as point of view shifts from the narrator's
objective description to the soldier's verbatim memory of the
incident.

During the first part of the narrative, in particular, while
the soldier is lucid, his conscious memory retains many events
verbatim. In such instances, he is transported back to the time
and the place at which the event occurred, so that it is reported as it happened, in the present tense. Drama slowly
builds impetus in the narrative until the soldier is shot. Then
the climactic scene during which he is shot is recounted in the
*passé composé,* and the rest of the story is narrated, for the
most part, in past tenses.

Events narrated in indirect discourse in the past tense often describe experiences through which the soldier passed unconsciously and which are later reported to him by someone else. Reporting them to him during his conscious moments relates them to the soldier's point of view. Close adherence to his point of view allows the narrative thread of *Dans le Labyrinthe* to founder between past and present events, which are partly experienced, partly remembered, and joined in misalliance by the feverish soldier. This adherence to his point of view leaves the soldier wandering in the labyrinth of living and dying, holding on to life even to the last, human in his stubborn obstinacy with regard to the box and finding its owner. Committed to his dead comrade throughout, the soldier is assailed by the physical events of war, disease, and the cold, and confused by encounters with other human beings. He is further confused by his own compulsions, paranoid fears, attempts to escape, to flee, and to communicate. The soldier becomes a poignant example of the individual striving toward life, even while continuously losing ground in the throes of certain death.

The temporal sequence is dependent upon the soldier's experience. Either the soldier's flashbacks interrupt his immediate experience or the narrator's inventive preoccupations intervene in his story, so that both the narrator and the soldier continually interrupt the narrative progression. Both perspectives mix perception and fantasy. The first part of the narrative consists mostly of perception, in contrast to the latter part, which, particularly after the shooting, founders in constant fantasies and feverish sequences of former events which impose themselves on the dying soldier. The imperfect and the *passé composé* proliferate, therefore, in the latter part of the narrative.

One kind of past tense specifically relevant to *Dans le Labyrinthe* is one I shall call the textual past since it refers uniquely to objects, characters, and events which have been alluded to previously in the text, but which do not completely materialize until described in the past tense. This is part of the creative process of the narrator's imagination.

Robbe-Grillet's narrator begins his fictional narrative slowly. There are many instances of hestitation and selection among three possibilities as the narrative takes shape in the mind of the narrator. Often the imperfect tense or the *passé composé* introduced in a recurring scene is the reader's first indication of which object, which character, or which event has been selected as the correct one to be incorporated into the narrative. The past tense in these instances is one normally referring to the former textual suggestion rather than to a chronological past occurrence.

In the initial introduction of an object on a table, for example, Robbe-Grillet first suggests vaguely that the figure of a cross on the table resembles a sort of table knife which might be either a flower, or a human figurine, or perhaps a dagger (p. 13). In the next paragraph, his focus shifts from this cross-like form, "dans la direction indiquée par la queue de la fleur, ou par la pointe du poignard"—thus reducing the choice to either flower or dagger—to another adjacent circular form. Six pages later he mentions an object on the mantel shaped like the same kind of cross with four appendages. This cross-like figure is reflected as well in the analogous motif of the wallpaper. The pattern of the wallpaper is smaller, however, and suggests a small flower, a single clove, or a miniature torch. It is in this last description that the narrator, and the author, reveal precisely the initial object which originally suggested this metamorphosing cross motif. By indicating in the past tense, in the imperfect in this instance, which one of the three initial suggestions accurately described the first form, the narrator reveals for the first time what object originally motivated his imagination. He reveals the original object in retrospect, so to speak. He describes the present reflection of the cross motif on the wallpaper by referring back to a dagger-bayonet, thereby choosing from among his original suggestions only the one which obtains and will continue to obtain throughout the novel.

C'est un papier gris pâle, rayé verticalement de bandes à peine plus foncées; entre les bandes foncées, au milieu de chaque bande claire, court une ligne de petits dessins, tours identiques, d'un gris très sombre: un fleuron, une espèce de clou de girofle, ou un minuscule flambeau, dont le manche est constitué par *ce qui était tout à l'heure la lame d'un poignard,* le manche de ce poignard figurant maintenant la flamme, et les deux appendices latéraux en forme de flamme, qui était la garde du poignard, représentant cette fois la petite coupe qui empêche les matières brûlantes de couler le long du manche.

[P. 19; italics mine]

This choice does not mean that the narrator will see the cross motif only as a dagger-bayonet throughout the remainder of the book. On the contrary, he continues developing the figure immediately on the following page as suggesting a kind of flashlight, since its top extremity is rounded like a light bulb rather than flamelike in form. This comparison obviously links the bayonet with the lamp in the room and with the street lamp against which the soldier often leans; but this kind of cross-reference of images in Robbe-Grillet has become a recognizable part of his particular style and is particularly appropriate in this novel for construing its "labyrinth." As one last note on the development of the cross motif, it is not until thirty-two pages later that it again reappears in the meticulous description of a cross within a circle imprinted in the snow by the boy's boot heel with its size indicated in the center of the cross (p. 56).[20]

As for characters in his narrative, the boy and the soldier similarly materialize in human form only after several allusions introduce the notion of a child and of a soldier.

A boy is first mentioned in passing while the narrator describes the half-opened door of a building through which the boy and the soldier eventually will pass. The half-opened door leaves "un intervalle assez large pour que s'y glisse un homme, ou du moins un enfant" (p. 21). Four pages later, in his first detailed description of the picture, the narrator mentions the boy: "Un gamin est assis à même le sol" (p. 25). But it is not until after several more descriptive pages of the picture that he suddenly comes to life. The narrator's gaze wanders off into fantasy as he begins weaving a story from the fixed elements before his eyes. The boy is the first to materialize from the picture as a human actor. He is first presented in negative contrast to the soldier's glance. As is frequently the case in this novel, negative enumeration suggests that what is not yet present will be present or that what does not yet occur will occur.[21] Any suggestion in the text, even if it is negative, might materialize. Just mentioning something in negative context gives it priority for realization and imprints itself on the reader's mind, so that upon occurrence for the first time, it seems to recur. Robbe-Grillet constantly evokes this effect of *déjà vu*. In the following passage, both the soldier and the boy are first mentioned negatively in order to place them on the stage for their dialogue.

Mais c'est comme si le soldat ne voyait pas l'enfant—ni l'enfant ni rien d'autre. Il a l'air de s'être endormi de fatigue, assis contre la table, les yeux grands ouverts.

C'est l'enfant qui prononce les premières paroles. Il dit: "Tu dors?" Il a parlé très bas, comme s'il craignait de réveiller le dormeur. Celui-ci n'a pas bronché. Au bout de quelques secondes, l'enfant répète, à peine un peu plus haut:

"Tu dors?" Et il ajoute, de la même voix neutre, légèrement chantante: "Tu peux pas dormir là, tu sais."

[P. 30]

It is usually upon the third suggestion that the object, or the character, materializes. Similarly to the presentation of the boy, the soldier is heard first only as a sound of heels on the pavement (p. 11), second, he appears as "une hanche, un bras, une épaule" (p. 16) leaning against a lamppost, and finally he materializes as "le soldat" who carries a package under his arm (p 20) Then he is included as one of the three soldiers in the picture (p. 26) before he takes part in the first dialogue of the narrative cited above.

At first he remains inanimate and scarcely able to speak until after the boy has prodded him several times with questions to which the soldier responds ambiguously, " 'Non . . . Oui . . . Je sais', dit le soldat" (p. 30). His lips do not move, at least the boy does not see them move, until the soldier's barely audible remark: " 'Ton père . . .' commence le soldat. Puis il s'arrête. Mais cette fois les lèvres ont légèrement remué" (p. 31).

In this first sketchy dialogue, the soldier and the boy situate each other within the fictional field by movement, by coming to life as puppets on a stage. Just preceding this dialogue, the narrator makes a long description of the picture in the *present* tense which terminates by a description of the soldier and the boy in the narrative *past*—or imperfect— tense. The narrator's visual perception, then, is recounted in the present, his imaginative creation of the story veers off into the imperfect.

The narrator is not situated in relation to what he imagines of the soldier. He is only situated at the beginning in the room, from which he draws elements out of which he spins the story of a dying soldier. While he is spinning the story, his point of view turns inward toward a descriptive narration of the soldier's actions in the past tense. Most of the time, however, he identifies with the soldier, or at least allows his soldier a kind of independent perspective which takes over his story, causing it to occur predominantly in the present tense. The soldier's own flashbacks sometimes interrupt his story, however, and sometimes the narrator interrupts it, bringing perspective back to the room and to his own creative imagination. In this beginning dialogue the switch from the narrator's perception to his imagination is clearly marked by a change of tense.

In each case the past tense materializes previous hypotheses suggested in the text. An event mentioned in the past has not necessarily occurred prior to the present narration of it, although it *may* have done so. An object or a person has not necessarily existed before its or his materialization by the successive stages outlined above.[22]

This kind of textual past serves a literary function whenever it appears. It is a past introduced primarily to stress the immediacy of the present tense even more vividly than a continually running present sequence could do. Such past-tense transitions or introductions to dialogues are frequent, particularly at the beginning of *Dans le Labyrinthe,* seeming at the very least to add esthetic distance to dramatic moments and to emphasize the immediate effect of verbal exchange.

In addition to this peculiar use of the past tense which I have termed a textual past, Robbe-Grillet also frequently allies past tenses with an inward-turning direction of his characters' thoughts, perceptions, and imaginations. Usually when a prolonged passage appears in the text in the past tense, it is safe to assume that perspective has turned inward, and that the world then described is one remembered or imagined.[23] This is not only true for past-tense transitions such as those outlined above, but can also be discerned in longer past-tense passages.

The following flashback on the part of the soldier, for example, consists of a transitional introduction in the imperfect tense, suggesting that he is remembering the scene which follows. As occurs frequently in the novel, this flashback begins with the word "et," indicating his shift from external perception to internal memory.

C'est cependant ce même gamin, à l'air sérieux, qui l'a conduit jusqu'au café tenu par l'homme qui n'est pas son père. *Et* c'était une scène semblable, sous un même lampadaire, à un carrefour identique. La neige tombait peut-être seulement avec un peu moins de violence. Les flocons étaient plus épais, plus lourds, plus lents. . . .                                          [P. 36; italics mine]

Although description of this remembered scene continues in the imperfect tense, its subsequent dialogue, which is also remembered, is reported in the present tense. As previously suggested, the spoken exchanges dramatize themselves in this way vividly and accurately within the soldier's memory as well as before the reader's eyes. Another short descriptive passage in the past follows the dialogue before returning to the present action of the narrative. This concluding description marks the end of the soldier's internal flashback before returning to his present perception of himself and the boy just entering the café.

Il n'est jamais, en tout cas, parvenu à aucun boulevard, à aucune voie plus large ou plantée d'arbres, ou différent en quoi que ce fût. L'enfant avait fini par préciser quelques noms, les quelques noms de rues qu'il connaissait, évidemment inutilisables.
Il tape maintenant son béret d'un geste vif contre le montant de bois.                                                                    [P. 38]

Since the soldier's point of view is contained within the narrator's, this entire passage can be read as the narrator's fantasy rather than the soldier's memory, or perhaps as the narrator's fantasy *and* the soldier's memory. In both cases, however, the past tenses here mark the inward-turning direction of the narrative toward memory and fantasy before returning to the present progression of the story.

Again marking a shift to internal memory, the following negative description occurs in the past. Rather than a flashback, this passage may be considered a "flashforward," to anglicize Bernard Pingaud's "retour en avant."[24] The soldier in the following passage thinks he may have passed in front of the barracks without seeing them; the kind of barracks he has *not* seen is subsequently described. This description is made in the present tense, but is followed by the soldier's denial of ever having seen a barracks of such classical structure. Much later in the novel (on page 184), another flashback of the soldier reveals that this is indeed the very barracks he has formerly seen where his comrade died. Since the reader of the following passage is not yet aware of the incident of his comrade's death, however, this earlier negative description seems obscure; it recalls a scene which has not yet been reported in the narrative. The scene is described in such detail that it seems to have already been experienced by the soldier in spite of his negations.

Sans s'en apercevoir, il est peut-être passé devant une caserne, au cours de ses pérégrinations. Cependant il n'a pas remarqué de bâtisse dans le style traditionnel: une construction basse . . . [description here in present tense].
Le soldat n'a rien vu de tel. Il n'a longé aucune grille; il n'a pas aperçu de vaste cour semée de gravier; il n'a rencontré ni feuillages touffus ni guérites, ni bien entendu de factionnaires en armes. Il n'a même pas emprunté le moindre boulevard planté d'arbres. Il n'a parcouru toujours que les mêmes rues rectilignes,

entre deux hautes files de façades plates; mais une caserne peut aussi revêtir cette apparence. Les guérites ont été enlevées, naturellement, ainsi que tout ce qui pouvait distinguer l'immeuble dans le série de ceux qui l'entourent; il ne subsiste que les barreaux de fer qui protègent les fenêtres. . . . **[Pp. 73–74]**

This description continues in the present tense, including this time details of the barracks which he does see and is passing. The precision of Robbe-Grillet's physical detail here parallels Camus's precision of physiological detail in the description of Meursault's imagining an eventual pardon. In both authors, the precision of objective description makes an impression of subjective experience on the reader.

Robbe-Grillet's most curious use of the past tense occurs at the climax of the soldier's story. The scenes of shooting the soldier and of bringing his body to the young woman's apartment are the two longest passages of the book narrated in the past tense.

In the first instance, the past tense is used to describe the soldier and the boy hiding from the enemy invader. The use of the past tense here is peculiar, since the action occurs during its description. Perhaps the narrator's perspective again takes over the narrative at this point, causing its action to occur in the past tense. Whether or not this is true, the dramatic effect of the scene is certainly enhanced by its unusual narration in the past. The suspense of the scene is toned down by its running past-tense description; at the same time, its drama is heightened by its lengthy contrast to the present-tense text which precedes and follows it.

The interesting contrast within this past-tense passage is its exceptionally short paragraph in the present tense describing the two enemy soldiers on their motorcycle. Since the passage is too long to quote in its entirety, its action might best be summarized and then followed by a short excerpt in order to demonstrate its dramatic effect.

The first warning of the approaching enemy is the distant sound of a motor which sets off description in the past tense. The boy urges the weary soldier to his feet and they both crouch together in a doorway in order to escape the ever-louder approaching motor. At the appearance of the enemy soldiers on their motorcycle, description of them suddenly switches to the present tense, lending them an ominous presence by contrast to the preceding past description. As long as the enemy soldiers are visible, description of them is made in the present tense. With their disappearance at the end of the street, the narrative returns to the past tense for the remainder of the incident at the end of which the soldier is shot, drags himself into hiding, and loses consciousness just as the boy discovers him. Either point of view has shifted to the narrator-doctor who watches this scene from afar and is narrating it as he witnessed it, as he imagines it occurred, or the past tense is again used for purely literary reasons, to emphasize this entire incident by contrasting tenses, that is. The following passage exemplifies the dramatic presence of the enemy soldiers when they become visible and description of them reverts to the present in the middle of action described in the past.

C'est alors qu'ils ont entendu le bruit, très lointain, de la motocyclette. Le gamin a, le premier, dressé l'oreille; il a ouvert la bouche un peu plus et sa tête a pivoté, graduellement. . . . C'était un side-car, monté par deux soldats casqués; il avançait au ralenti, au milieu de la chaussée, dans la neige intacte.

Les deux hommes se présentent de profil. Le visage du conducteur, situé en avant, est à un niveau plus élevé que celui de son compagnon, assis en contre-bas sur le siège latéral. Ils ont sensiblement les même traits tous les deux. . . .

Ils sont passés sans se retourner, et ils ont continué tout droit, après le carrefour. Au bout d'une vingtaine de mètres, ils ont disparu derrière l'angle de l'immeuble formant le coin d'en face.                                                    [Pp. 164–70]

The present-tense description of the soldiers is based upon direct perception of them, whereas the past-tense description relates the action of this scene. The enemy presence silences the hustle and conversation preceding their arrival; the present description of them occurs at the moment they become visible, thus simulating the calm center of a whirling tornado during which the weight of their concrete presence cannot be avoided.

Beginning at this point in the narrative, the past tenses proliferate as the soldier nears death. As he progressively loses his grasp of reality and passes through longer periods of unconsciousness, the action narrated in the past correlates with his losing touch with life. Intermittently his moments of lucidity appear as detailed present descriptions of the room or of the characters surrounding him. Sometimes he joins together, in the present tense, disconnected flashbacks which relate to his present surroundings, in a desperate effort to hold on to life. He frantically and obsessively describes his surroundings in detail in order to stay alive until the very last, when his final glance moves from the table leg upward to the table top, and from there further upward toward the ceiling as his eyes close in death. Robbe-Grillet's visual bias is impossible to escape.

Many past-tense passages included in this final section of the soldier's narrative summarize long speeches related to him in indirect discourse but which are here set off only by a tense change. These range from short interjections of another character's speech to longer reports constituting an entire incident. The following example of this use of the past tense demonstrates that here the past does refer to an anterior event, but one which is reported to the soldier for the first time by the woman.

La jeune femme, elle, n'a pas bougé de sa chaise; et elle répond sans trop se faire prier, sans doute pour que le blessé se tienne tranquille. C'est l'enfant qui est venu lui dire que le soldat dont elle s'était occupée la veille gisait sans connaissance, dans une entreé de maison, à quelques rues de chez eux, recroquevillé sur lui-même, ne parlant plus, n'entendant rien, ne remuant pas plus que s'il était mort. Elle avait aussitôt décidé de s'y rendre. Un homme se trouvait déjà près du corps, un civil, qui passait à ce moment, par hasard, disait-il, mais qui semblait en fait avoir assisté de loin à toute la scène. . . .          [Pp. 198–201]

In short, Robbe-Grillet uses tense to create numerous ambiguities of his labyrinth. As long as the narrator hesitantly formulates his narrative, the choices of tense are multiple and at first seem to confound past and present. Once we are into the narrative, however, the soldier's perspective determines tense, in that even if an event has chronologically preceded the moment at which it is reported, the narrative nevertheless remains in the present tense, faithfully reporting the event as present to the soldier's vision. In general, therefore, the action takes place in the present as do the dialogues and, in many instances, as does recall, though any of these may appear in the past in a seemingly arbitrary fashion.

Although the past sometimes serves to report chronologically anterior events, it principally serves literary purposes of transition, of dramatic contrast, and of correlation with the soldier's half-conscious states as death approaches. The appearance of the past tense in the *Labyrinthe* indicates an inward-turning of perspective toward memory and fantasy, or it indicates a climactic moment in the story rather than an anterior moment as is normally expected. In this sense, the past serves purely an esthetic rather than a temporal function in *Dans le Labyrinthe*.

### Narrative scenes

Finally, a number of sentences in the *Labrinthe* which glare out of context, apparently unrelated to the passages in which they are found, have a common denominator: they constitute a theatrical vision fundamental to the book's conception. By "theatrical vision" I mean the pictorial evocation of a background décor against which characters play a role; these two elements usually combine to form a "scene," one of which follows the other in a sequence dependent upon a single perspective. This basic vision, or way of seeing, is shared by the narrator and the soldier.

This theatrical skeleton unites a number of statements which patently break out of fictional context, and clarifies as well some of the fundamental elements which determine perspective throughout. It suggests, for example, that *Dans le*

*Labyrinthe* might have been written originally as a film scenario in which the camera could double for its visual perspective; this would account for its eternal present and its many enigmas which refer to scenes not included because they occur offstage, as it were. And lastly, the uncertainty of its sequence of scenes as well as their repetition and recurrence could very well derive from the photographic method of cutting and splicing. In addition, the general construction of the novel fits easily into the basic categories of classical French drama: *Dans le Labyrinthe* begins with a clear-cut exposition, followed by its development leading to the climactic shooting and death of the soldier, and terminates with the doctor-narrator's dénouement which clarifies the preceding dramatic series of scenes. The entire narrative recounts the single tragic event of the soldier's death which occurs within twenty-four hours against the single décor of the city.

The narrator in this theatrical sense would be the *metteur en scène,* and the soldier, the actor, although they both share visual observation as their common fundamental method of participation. Their perspectives are based upon a visual sequence of pictorial scenes. Both the narrator and the soldier see series of scenes which are described for the most part, and interspersed with dialogue as a kind of dramatic relief. Transition from object to object, or from scene to scene, is often accomplished by the displacement indicated by a glance, by the pointing finger, or by the itinerary of a character. Reflection and repetition determine events and their development. Gesture leads up to the climactic freezing, or stasis, of the pictorial scene rather than to the kinesis of dramatic action. Frequent repetition of a single scene contrasted with a second scene, as applied in *L'Anné dernière à Marienbad* by black and white contrasts, builds dramatic tension, and frozen scenes in which all action is stopped indicate climactic moments.

Evidence of this theatrical skeleton upon which Robbe-Grillet, and his narrator, construct the soldier's drama is found throughout the novel.

In his exposition preceding the narrative, the narrator

initially describes the city as a lifeless décor against which he chooses certain characters from the picture on his wall to act out the drama. In beginning his description of the snowy landscape, the narrator compares its two-dimensional aspect to a poorly painted picture on a blank wall. Such a comparison suggests both the derivation of the landscape from the picture in his room and his imagined composition of the city while staring at his blank wall.

. . . la neige qui continue de tomber étant au paysage tout son relief, comme si cette vue brouillée était seulement mal peinte, en faux-semblant, contre un mur nu                    [P. 15]

Later he summarizes his first description by suggesting that the scenery is now in place, but that the stage as yet is empty.

La platitude de tout ce décor ferait croire, d'ailleurs, qu'il n'y a rien derrière ces façades. Et toute la scène demeure vide: sans un homme, ni une femme, ni même un enfant.          [P. 24]

Although there is no personal reference to the narrator in the first sentence of this passage, the second one summarizes all he has described up to this point in a single interpretive sentence attributable only to the person telling the story. Only the narrator's perspective could envisage the entire city as a stage, or even as a single scene, empty as yet of characters. The negative suggestion, as usual in this work, impresses upon the reader what is to follow. This passage serves as a transition to the picture, which is then described in detail, including specifically the soldier and the boy, who eventually begin to speak, to move, and to animate the city scene. The structure of the narrative consists thereafter of alternate sequences of description, which sets the stage, and dialogue, which reveals the events of the narrative.

This initial description of the empty stage is reflected in a scene near the end of the narrative just preceding the soldier's death when he sees around his deathbed all the actors first introduced as absent:

Autour de lui se tiennent trois personnages, debout, immobiles,

qui le regardent sans rien dire: un homme, une femme et un
enfant.                                                    [P. 181]

Between these two passages appears a similar passage.
Both its structure and its content reflect the two passages cited
above in Robbe-Grillet's familiar technique of reinforcing the
*déjà vu* by repetition. Emphasis upon the dramatic is evident
enough in the following passage, although it is a scene frozen
in place. The last sentence is the one which suggests comparison and contrast with the two former passages. Again it
interprets, again it stands out of context except by reference
to the dramatic schema, again it prophesies what is to follow,
and again it describes the man, the woman, and the child.

Un bras reste à moitié levé, une bouche entrouverte, une tête
penchée à la renverse; mais la tension a succédé au mouvement,
les traits se sont crispés, les membres raidis, le sourire est
devenu rictus, l'élan a perdu son intention et son sens. Il ne
subsiste plus, à leur place, que la démesuré, et l'étrangeté, et la
mort.                                                      [P. 110]

All of these "frozen" scenes, in which movement stops,
suggest not only high points of the narrative expressed by one
of Robbe-Grillet's favorite techniques, but also in this novel
foreshadow the eventual death of the soldier, and refer even
more directly to the picture, *The Defeat of Reichenfels*. Robbe-
Grillet catches important scenes in still-shots in order to mark
moments of dramatic import. This scene repeats a previous
one in which the man, woman, and child are frozen by the
soldier's look in the midst of their gestures (p. 91).

Another passage which stands out of context refers to
the title of the picture, *The Defeat of Reichenfels,* and does so
specifically, but in the most objective, and, certainly at first
reading, enigmatic terms which are never clarified. By paral-
leling this scene, which describes the entrance of the soldier
and the boy into the café, with other descriptions of the picture, this sentence clearly refers to the actual title of the actual
picture found in the narrator's room as if it could be read in
the faces of the clientele in the café. Ben Stoltzfus has pointed
out that Robbe-Grillet originally intended this title to be that

of the entire book as well as the picture in the book, and undoubtedly the general atmosphere of the narrative is one of defeat.[25] Again, this scene is static and therefore surprises by its introduction of a sentence spoken by figures which are frozen. The overlapping of the two domains, however, the soldier's becoming that of the narrator by a kind of verbal montage, affords the greatest shock.

Le gamin se trouvait encore près de la porte, à cet instant, derrière son dos. Mais les autres en face de lui demeuraient figés, la bouche fermée, les lèvres immobiles; *et la phrase,* sans personne pour l'avoir prononcée, *semblait être une légende au bas d'un dessin.*                              [P. 147; italics mine]

Only by suddenly abstracting perspective from the soldier in the middle of this last sentence, and by subsequently attributing it to the narrator is one able to visualize the scene from a distance as the entire picture referred to with the title written under it, *The Defeat of Reichenfels.*[26]

A number of passages also stand out of context which use the word *scène* in its connotation of a scene in a drama. In other words, events of the narrative are conceived as scenes which have preceded or which will follow other scenes. In some instances, moreover, the word "scene" confirms the theatrical conception of *Dans le Labyrinthe* even more strongly by signifying "stage," as if characters are sometimes onstage or offstage, depending upon their momentary presence in the novel. (All italics mine.)

Le soldat fait en tout cas semblant de ne pas avoir remarqué sa rentrée en scène.                                                [P. 50]

Cette scène se serait-elle déroulée hors de sa presence?      [P. 91]

En même temps s'est arrêté le mouvement d'horlogerie qui faisait entendre son tic-tac régulier, sans que le soldat en ait pris con-science, depuis le début de *la scène.*
    Et c'est *sur une scène muette* que la lumière se rallume. Le décor est sensiblement le même.                              [P. 100]

*L'image suivante* représente la chambrée d'une caserne. . . .
                                                                [P. 161]

C'est sans doute à cet endroit que se place *la scène de l'assemblée muette* qui s'écarte en tous sens, autour de lui, le soldat demeurant à la fin seul au centre d'un immense cercle de visages blêmes. . . . Mais cette scène ne mène à rien.                    [P. 179]

Non. C'est en réalité un autre blessé qui *occupe la scène,* à la sortie du café.                                             [P. 182]

C'est à ce moment, seulement, qu'il s'étonne d'être de retour dans cette pièce, qui appartient *à une scène* très antérieure.
                                                                      [P. 193]

Pourtant *la scène suivante* le représente dans le lit. . . .    [P. 201]

In his last half-conscious moments the soldier perceives his surroundings in theatrical terms, clearly described as melodrama during his conscious moments, and vaguely alluded to as nightmare during his unconscious moments.

Bien que le fond de leur désaccord ne soit pas facile à démêler, la violence en est indiquée suffisamment par *le maintien des antagonistes,* qui se livrent l'un comme l'autre à des *gesticulations démonstratives,* prennent des *attitudes théâtrales,* font des *mimiques exagérées* . . . afin de suivre des dernières *péripéties* qui menacent de devenir dramatiques, tout en se cachant quand même les yeux derrière ses mains, *étalées en écran devant son visage.*                                             [P. 202]

Viennent ensuite des *scènes moins claires*—encore plus fausses, aussi, probablement—*violentes,* quoique le plus souvent *muettes.* Elles ont pour théâtre des *lieux moins précis,* moins caractérisés, plus impersonnels.                         [Pp. 202–3; italics mine]

Finally the narrator-doctor sums up his account of the narrative by designating each of the main characters as having played a certain role in the now-completed narrative-drama.[27] In summarizing these roles, the narrator seems to be looking at the picture as his description passes from one character to the other.

La femme qui a soigné le soldat blessé n'a tiré de lui aucun renseignement, quant à son camarade mort avant lui. . . . Son fils, un enfant d'une dizaine d'années au visage sérieux, l'avait rencontré auparavant dans la rue, peut-être même à plusieurs reprises. . . . Son rôle est primordial puisque c'est lui, par son imprudence, qui a déclenché l'action des occupants du side-car, mais ses nombreuses apparitions ne sont pas toutes déterminantes au même degré. L'invalide, en revanche, ne joue pratiquement aucun rôle. . . . Le patron de café, pour sa part, est énigmatique, ou insignifiant. Il ne dit pas un seul mot, ne fait pas un seul geste. . . . Les comparses qui discutent devant lui avec tant d'animation ne lui apprendront rien. . . . Le soldat . . . possède certainement une vue plus réaliste des combats; aussi n'a-t-il rien à dire à leur sujet; il doit être seulement en train d'attendre qu'on lui serve à boire. . . .                                            [Pp. 217–18]

At the last, upon completing his description of the soldier, the narrator again falls victim to his tale-telling imagination and seemingly takes up his narrative again, beginning once more from the café scene, with the only difference being the weather in the city outside the café.

This concept of scene indicates that Robbe-Grillet's temporal sequence in *Dans le Labyrinthe* is based upon a sequence of static scenes. At certain moments purely spatial configurations or parts of events which alone the soldier has experienced or "seen" are recalled in chaotic order. Recurrence, whether total or partial, mental or physical, is emphasized by Robbe-Grillet's peculiar spatial orientation.[28] Recurrence of a scene with slight variation, whole or partial as the case may be, constitutes his phenomenal world. Fictional progression consists of recall of former places and events altered only slightly, one following the other arbitrarily on a single plane. Yet there is progression, and progression with such a residue of familiar experience constantly enlarged by new elements that the tempo remains slow and the events overlap one another in a sequence which remains spiral at best.

The spiral figure, in fact, recurs frequently throughout the novel. Even at the last, the narrator begins again his same narrative, though it takes place in the rain rather than in the snow this second time. Yet he "leaves the city behind him!" (p. 221). Whether he leaves behind him the narrative, or the book, or life itself, remains inconclusive, the final great enigma posed by Robbe-Grillet's entire labyrinthine world. He does take a step forward, however, and rids himself of this fictional

spiraling world in a way which suggests, nevertheless, its infinite recurrence.


## The archetypal labyrinth

The frequent appearance in current French literary criticism of the term "labyrinth" to designate almost any New
Novel or aspects thereof suggests that it is more than merely
appropriate in a literary sense. Besides expressing the puzzle
or detective-story aspect of New Novels in general, and of
Robbe-Grillet's novels in particular, *Dans le Labyrinthe* represents a labyrinth in and of itself. Rather than expose a
labyrinthine novel to the reader, Robbe-Grillet literally imposes his labyrinth on the reader in the sense of ludic challenge
noted above. But above and within and beyond these purely
literary aspects of the *Labyrinthe,* elements of the labyrinthe
myth appeal profoundly to the collective unconscious, and
prove all the more disturbing and mystifying in this novel because they appear only in fragments of the traditional myth,
which is reversed and incomplete.

The Theseus myth is fragmented in *Dans le Labyrinthe*
like the Oedipus myth in Robbe-Grillet's first novel *Les
Gommes.* Clues strewn throughout the text such as the forgotten street the soldier eternally seeks "–na–" might well refer
to Minotaur Street as he often strives to recall: "Mallart,
Malardier, Montoire, Moutardier. . . . Non, ça ne ressemblait
pas à cela" (95). The young woman who at the last knits
beside the soldier's deathbed suggests an Ariadne peaceably
knitting her thread rather than leading Theseus out of the
labyrinth. The crack on the ceiling of the dying soldier's room
also resembles a string leading him out of the maze. Just as
B. Morrissette reads "Daulis" unscrambled to reveal "Laius"
in *Les Gommes,* one might stretch the name of the dead owner
of the box, Henri Martin, to read "Minotaure" in the *Labyrinthe.* The obsessive description of the marble in his pocket

given to the boy by the soldier suggests an eye; perhaps it is the eye of the monster-bull, Minotaur, rather than, or as well as, a blackball signifying death, as one critic has surmised.[29]

But all these instances, singly or grouped together, neither clearly complete the traditional myth nor do they seem clearly to create a new one in its place. This is so consistent with Robbe-Grillet's usual practice that even as lucid a critic as John Sturrock has been led to remark: "[Robbe-Grillet] is not prepared to allow anything even approaching a coherent fantasy to develop, which would be equivalent to a new metaphysic, an established myth by which to interpret subsequent events in the phenomenal world."[30] Yet, after likening this novel to "that baroque artefact which Robbe-Grillet might adopt as a blazon, the labyrinth," Mr. Sturrock goes on to qualify Robbe-Grillet's labyrinth in the following terms:

But those who set out to penetrate to the heart of an actual labyrinth are kept going by the knowledge that there *is* a correct path, if only they can find it. The hero of a Robbe-Grillet novel shares the same ambition, but what in real life is knowledge is in his case illusion, for if there were a path to the centre of the labyrinth then he would be able to impose a final order in his troubled world. As far as Robbe-Grillet is concerned, to do this in our own day and age is a preposterous ambition, and it is therefore one that he must show to be doomed even as it takes shape. . . . The progress of the narrator who tries to follow them and link them together into a coherent townscape or piece of architecture represents the will to find comfort in a definitive order of things. But the motion which Robbe-Grillet permits is only brief and fragmentary, each section of street, corridor, or the like, being simply the evidence of the mind's frustration. . . . But Robbe-Grillet is asking us to work on his novels in order to understand them, and to treat them as phenomenological objects, unverifiable but open to our investigations, and sure to reflect our own myths back at us if we fail to extract their true measurements.[31]

Although Mr. Sturrock clearly underlines the central importance of the figure of the labyrinth to Robbe-Grillet's creative endeavor here, he sees it only as brief and fragmentary and thereby antipathetic to the establishment of a more comprehensive myth. By a slight change of emphasis, by accepting the double perspective which separates the narrator from the soldier and the clarity of the creative process from the confusion of its created world, I think Mr. Sturrock would agree that Robbe-Grillet does create his own peculiar myth of the labyrinth which is not only reiterated in all of his works, as Mr. Sturrock and others have suggested, but which becomes particularly germane to this novel as the most cogent *mise en oeuvre* of the author's obsessive concern. By separating the narrator from the soldier, the clarity of the creative process from the confusion of its created fiction, one understands that, far from trying to find his way *into* the labyrinth, Robbe-Grillet as creator—and narrator—*is already in the center of the labyrinth.*

The initial sentence placing the narrator solidly in the center of the room reveals Robbe-Grillet's notion that the author finds himself in the center trying to wend his way *out* of rather than *into* the labyrinth. The spatial or essentially scenic orientation of the novel further suggests the passive and solid, stable, unchanging location of the narrator in a room which clearly delineates his solid, concrete, and stable location at the center (or in the head, as Mr. Sturrock surmises) of a room representing the creative consciousness from which the labyrinthine world—unstable, changing and confusing—of the soldier's wandering toward death is reflected, imagined, or created. Robbe-Grillet as writer and artist finds himself already in the created solid reality of the room, microcosm of the imagined or dreamed fictional world. His creation of the room and its reflected city together form the macrocosm of our real world which must evolve from a stable central microcosm.

In short, I see this novel as a desperate attempt of certain elements of the collective unconscious to express themselves through Robbe-Grillet in order to put an end to chaos and enigma or ambiguity by making of that ambiguity a single, total, and unified image which includes in its configuration numerous enigmatic dead ends, negations, twistings, and turn-

ings of the archetypal labyrinth. The *Labyrinthe* contains
hints of classical traits fleetingly suggested which tend toward
harmony, equilibrium, order, and measure just as the Manner-
ist and baroque writers of the sixteenth and seventeenth centuries hinted at the ensuing age of classical harmony. Robbe-
Grillet makes a desperate attempt to reestablish the equilibrium
of the spatial center which will resolve all discord and lack of
measure. He attempts to silence cacaphony and clamor and to
reestablish the still center without circumference, the limitless
and eternal calm of being without doing or acting or even
saying.

In Jungian terms, Robbe-Grillet's labyrinth represents
a mandala image in which diversity and adversity are encom-
passed in a single unified figure:

A circular image of this kind compensates the disorder and confusion of the psychic state—namely, through the construction of
a central point to which everything is related, or by a concentric
arrangement of the disordered multiplicity and of contradictory
and irreconcilable elements. This is evidently an attempt at self-
healing on the part of Nature . . . from an instinctive impulse. . . .
Mandalas represent concentration, and self-immersion, for the
purpose of realizing inner experience. . . . At the same time they
serve to produce an inner order. . . . They express the idea of a
safe refuge, of inner reconciliation and wholeness.[32]

Passing reference might be made in this respect to the
clear line of contemporary thinking in French letters which
sees the twentieth-century experience of time as best expressed
by the present beginning, say, with Bergson and Proust and
evolving through Sartre and his fellow "committed" authors of
the postwar period. It does not seem accidental that the
French critic Georges Poulet, who traces the contemporary
avatars of present time, also writes on the metamorphoses of
the circle, or that Gaston Bachelard's notion of the labyrinth
as conceived by the poetic mind both add to this figure as being
one central to the contemporary creative mentality. But present artistic preoccupation with the labyrinth is not exclusively
French. In Europe as well as America, recurring evidence of
artistic preoccupation with the labyrinth as an esthetic entity

ranges from single instances—such as the dance presentation of *labryinths* by the Polish Mime Theater or the recent critical commentary on the novel entitled *Circles without Center*—to entire fictional works—such as that of Jorge Luis Borges—in which the labyrinth constantly serves as a primary and central motif.[33]

Borges's tale entitled "The Garden of Forking Paths," in particular, contains nearly every fictional element found in Robbe-Grillet's *Labyrinthe,* although Borges's work dwindles in typical fashion to the concise proportions of a parable. Borges works by example, keeping his linear *récit* intact; Robbe-Grillet eclipses his linear *récit* by weaving fragments of it within the fabric of his tortuous labyrinthine text. Borges himself claims "The Garden of Forking Paths" to be a detective story, and, although the art of suspense which he constructs with quite as much artifice as Robbe-Grillet is fundamental to both authors, it can hardly be claimed to be his central concern. Borges's labyrinth, more clearly and lyrically than Robbe-Grillet's, suggests an infinite cosmos which reduces time to the *present* and space to the *presence* of the labyrinth:

I thought of a labyrinth of labyrinths, of one sinuous spreading labyrinth that would encompass the past and future and in some way involve the stars.[34]

The learned oriental Ts'ui Pên of Borges's fiction retires from an active, productive, committed life in order to write a book and to construct a labyrinth which, precisely as in Robbe-Grillet's *Labyrinthe,* prove to be one and the same. It is the fiction, however, and the "abysmal problem of time" which in reality most preoccupies Ts'ui Pên, the narrator, the interpreter Albert, and surely Borges himself, in this work.

Ts'ui Pên's handling of time in his novel precisely delineates the evolution from the Sartrean existential choice of a single time encompassing a clear, linear, chronological *récit* to Robbe-Grillet's ambiguous opening-out of multiple possible times simultaneously experienced:

In all fictional works, each time a man is confronted with several alternatives, he chooses one and eliminates the others; in the fiction of Ts'ui Pên, he chooses—simultaneously—all of them.[35]

The ancient Ts'ui Pên even resembles Robbe-Grillet in leaving out of his novel the single most important word which would serve as a key to its significance. Borges explains the import of such omissions in the following way:

"In a riddle whose answer is chess, what is the only prohibited word?"
I thought a moment and replied, "The word *chess*."
"Precisely," said Albert. *"The Garden of Forking Paths* is an enormous riddle, or parable, whose theme is time; this recondite cause prohibits its mention. To omit a word always, to resort to inept metaphors and obvious periphrases, is perhaps the most emphatic way of stressing it."[36]

Robbe-Grillet similarly omits key words such as "Minotaur" in this novel, and he closely allies his labyrinth to an unspoken theme of time, one which parallels that of Ts'ui Pên, and ultimately, of Borges himself:

*The Garden of Forking Paths* is an incomplete, but not false, image of the universe as Ts'ui Pên conceived it. In contrast to Newton and Schopenhauer, [he] did not believe in a uniform, absolute time. He believed in an infinite series of times, in a growing dizzying net of divergent, convergent and parallel times. This network of times which approached one another, forked, broke off, or were unaware of one another for centuries, embraces *all* possibilities of time.[37]

Another of Borges's tales, "The House of Asterion," was originally inspired by a painting of the mythical Minotaur inside the labyrinth looking out for a Theseus who never appears.[38] Robbe-Grillet's soldier in the center of the labyrinth woven by the narrator is similarly condemned.

But the most telling evidence of the archetypal character of Robbe-Grillet's labyrinth emerges from Mircea Eliade's description of the specific elements at work in creating such a myth *sub specie aeternitatis*. The exactitude with which Eliade spells out the precise elements at work in creating every labyrinthine myth seems to be concretely realized, though inadvertently so, by Robbe-Grillet's *Labyrinthe*. In general, Eliade attributes the labyrinthine myth to the universal need for creating sacred space—and eclipsing time in the process—in the form of temple, palace, or "centre of the world":

This symbolism of the centre . . . is as much involved in the building of towns as of houses: . . . every "construction," and every contact with a "centre" involves doing away with profane time, and entering the mythical *illud tempus* of creation. . . . Without being over-hasty in deciding the original meaning and function of labyrinths, there is no doubt that they included the notion of defending a "centre."[39]

In the primitive mind, such a "centre" town or city is surrounded by a labyrinth in order to foil incursions of spirits from without, especially evil spirits and even death itself. Eliade's notion of ritual initiation into the archetypal labyrinth when applied to Robbe-Grillet's text affords startling insight:

The labyrinth rituals upon which initiation ceremonies are based are intended . . . to teach the neophyte, during his sojourn on earth, how to enter the domains of death without getting lost.[40]

Robbe-Grillet in *Dans le Labyrinthe* simulates a ritual world of death for his neophyte-reader as for his neophyte-narrator in order to allow each, "during his sojourn on earth, to enter the domains of death without getting lost." The narrator does so by creating the fictional account of the "domain of death" which he leaves behind at the last without "getting lost," and the reader does likewise merely by reading the novel. Eliade projects this labyrinthine journey to every human life lived in every age, thus making of it a universal experience constantly reexperienced by each individual:

The journey to the "centre" is fraught with obstacles, and yet every city, every temple, every house *is* at the centre of the universe. The supreme rite of initiation is to enter a labyrinth and return from it, and yet every life, even the least eventful, can be taken as the journey through a labyrinth.[41]

It is with Eliade's further interpretation of the labyrinthine "centre" as a religious experience of sacred space transcending the merely temporal that many of Robbe-Grillet's admirers would undoubtedly take issue. Even in this respect, however, Robbe-Grillet's constant insistence on forms of all kinds suggests the longing or nostalgia spelled out by Eliade:

However different sacred space may be from profane, man cannot live except in this sort of sacred space. And when there is no hierophany to reveal it to him, he constructs it for himself according to the laws of cosmology and geomancy. . . . What seems to me significant is not the fact that the archetype is open to crude imitations (repetitions), but the fact that man *tends,* even at the lowest levels of his "immediate" religious experience, to draw near to this archetype and make it present. If this does reveal to us something about man's place in the cosmos it is not the fact that the Tree of Life can be abased to fit any magico-medical superstition, nor that the symbol of the centre can be reduced to such an "easy substitute" as the home; no; it is the need that man constantly feels to "realize" archetypes even down to the lowest and most "impure" levels of his immediate existence; it is this longing for transcendent forms—in this instance, for sacred space.[42]

Elsewhere, Eliade has called this longing the "'nostalgia for paradise,' the desire to be, permanently without effort, and even to some extent unconsciously, in a supremely sacred zone."[43] Even though Robbe-Grillet's *Labyrinthe* might not represent precisely what one normally envisions as "paradise," or even a "supremely sacred zone," it is his "longing" or "nostalgia" for, his urge toward establishing, such a calm and stable center which exercises such a powerful attraction for the contemporary artistic sensibility and which serves at the same time as its most cogent literary prototype.

By calling up the powerful archetype of the labyrinth as a figure which incorporates chaos within order, by resorting to a theatrical framework which promotes sequences of scenes emphasizing spatial at the expense of temporal coherence, by exploiting reflection both as a literary technique and as a profound esthetic conviction, Robbe-Grillet tries to impose the experience of creating fiction on the individual reader. Robbe-Grillet's vision begins with peace from within the calm center of each individual who, when exposed to the chaotic confusion of life or death or even the unconscious, will find his own individual solution. In fact, if Robbe-Grillet has a philosophy of life and death, an analogy-myth through which the labyrinthine complexity of life and death is to become comprehensible, it is only that there are no valid generic myths—each man's solution is *sui generis* and is arrived at through the static peace in his inner self.

# NOTES

## Introduction

1. The New Novel emphatically returns to the original principles underlying James's notion of point of view as outlined by Percy Lubbock in 1921 rather than adhering to the myriad ways in which this technique has been transformed by the academic criticism of the last fifty years. The American New Critics in particular juggled point of view into scarcely recognizable versions of James's original notion. Norman Friedman's article entitled "Point of View in Fiction: the Development of a Critical Concept" (*PMLA*, 70 [Dec. 1955]) remains a classic example of the extent to which preoccupation with point of view invaded critical thought in the United States by 1951. Wayne Booth's *Rhetoric of Fiction* (Chicago U. P., 1961) ten years later provided the inevitable antidote and rebuttal to scholarly extremism of this sort.

2. Percy Lubbock, *The Craft of Fiction* (New York: Viking, 1926; reissued 1957), p. 62.

3. Jean Ricardou, *Pour une Théorie du nouveau roman,* Coll. "Tel Quel" (Paris: Seuil, 1971), p. 264.

4. John Sturrock, *The French New Novel* (London: Oxford U. P., 1969), p. 29.

5. See especially Gérard Genette, "Vertige fixé," *Figures* (Paris: Seuil, 1966), and Ricardou, p. 262.

6. *Sewanee Review,* 52 (1945): 221–41, 435–56, 643–53.

7. Stephen Heath, *The Nouveau Roman* (Philadelphia: Temple U. P., 1972), p. 26.

8. *Homo Ludens* (Boston: Beacon Press, 1950).

9. Heath, p. 125.

10. Sturrock, p. 21.

11. Ibid., p. 22.

12. Ibid., p. 39.

13. The baroque is often invoked with regard to various aspects of the New Novel, but for a particularly brilliant and precise exposition of this interdependent notion, see Ricardou.

## Chapter 1

1. Jean-Paul Sartre, "M. François Mauriac et la liberté," *Situations I* (Paris: Gallimard, 1947), p. 48. (First published 1939).

2. Ibid.

3. Ibid., p. 16.

4. Ibid., p. 78.

5. Ibid., p. 120.

6. Ibid., p. 121.

7. Ibid. Situations II, p. 201.

8. Jean Pouillon, *Temps et roman* (Paris: Gallimard, 1946).

9. The word "modalities" originates with Bruce Morrissette, who discusses it most extensively in his article "De Stendhal à Robbe-Grillet: Modalités du 'point de vue,' " *Cahiers de l'Association Internationale des Études Françaises,* 14 (June 1962), 143–63.

10. Nathalie Sarraute, *L'Ère du soupçon* (Paris: Gallimard, 1950).

11. Ibid., p. 73.

12. Morrissette.

13. Wilbur Frohock, *Style and Temper* (Cambridge: Harvard U. P., 1967).

14. Jean Alter, "Essais sur le XXe siècle," *L'Esprit créateur,* 9:4 (winter 1968), 306.

15. Alain Robbe-Grillet, "Notes sur la localisation et les déplacements de point de vue dans la description romanesque," *Cinéma et roman,* 36–38, *La Revue des lettres modernes* (summer 1958).

16. Ibid., 257.

17. Robbe-Grillet, *Pour un nouveau Roman* (Paris: Editions de Minuit, 1963), p. 130.

18. Ibid.

19. Ibid., p. 131.

20. Ibid., p. 133.

21. Ibid., p. 134.

22. Olga Bernal, *Alain Robbe-Grillet: Le Roman de l'absence* (Paris: Gallimard, 1964), p. 173.

23. Michel Butor, "L'Usage des pronoms personnels dans le roman," *Répertoire II* (Paris: Gallimard, 1964), p. 63.

24. Ibid., p. 72.

25. Ricardou.

26. Morrissette, 148.

27. Robert Champigny, *Le Genre romanesque* (Monte-Carlo: Regain, 1963), p. 18.

28. Ricardou divides these two moments into "temps de la fiction et temps de la narration." Sturrock calls them "cosmic time and phenomenal time."

29. See Emily Zants, *Aesthetics of the New Novel in France* (Boulder, Colo.: U. Colo. P., 1968).

30. Frohock denies there are epiphanies in the New Novel. Alter claims that new configurations of objects and forms do constitute epiphanies.

31. Frohock's notion runs counter to the general orientation of spatial configurations as originally proposed by Frank and by my own Introduction to this text, among others.

32. Jean Bloch-Michel, *Le Présent de l'indicatif* (Paris: Gallimard, 1963).

33. Sturrock, p. 29.

34. This aspect of the New Novel is outlined in detail in my Introduction.

35. Sartre's preface to Nathalie Sarraute, *Portrait d'un inconnu* (Paris: Gallimard, 1959).

36. Sturrock, p. 4.

37. Ricardou, p. 18.

38. Sturrock, p. 25.

39. Ibid., p. 134ff.

40. Ibid., p. 17.

# Chapter 2

1. For a full portrait of the Sartrean anti-Semite, see Sartre, *Reflexions sur la question juive* (Paris: Gallimard, 1954, dans la Collection Idées).

Although Lucien is his fictional counterpart, it is important to see, with Claude-Edmonde Magny, that Lucien is more than *just* an anti-Semite.

La satire de *L'Enfance d'un chef* a un caractère sinistre; . . . Elle est trop inquiétante pour cela, parce qu'elle porte sur l'humain lui-même, et non sur l'un de ses aspects plus ou moins gauches ou ridicules, comme l'antisémitisme ou les associations "estudiantines" d'Action Française. Sartre y dépasse la satire sociale, la satire de "moeurs" autant que Swift dépasse Voltaire; et à cause de cela, il nous inquiète profondément; nous sentons trop que l'existence même de notre liberté, notre "dignité de roseau pensant," est ici mise en question. [*Les Sandales d'Empédocle* (Neuchâtel: Eds. de la Baconnière, 1945), p. 142]

2. Page references, hereafter following quotations, are to Sartre, "L'Enfance d'un chef" in *Le Mur* (Paris: Gallimard, 1939).

3. Certain critics find that Sartre often develops themes, such as *mensonge* in this story, too obviously. They maintain that by doing so, Sartre contradicts his literary theory and reveals his presence in his novels, thus his omniscience as author. Development of such themes seems here, rather, intrinsic to the development of Lucien's maturation process, especially in the light of Sartre's philosophical notion that every man's life has a theme, a project, or choice-of-being. *Mensonge* would constitute one of Lucien's fundamental modes of

being. Furthermore, orienting fiction around certain themes or figures, and reiteration of these themes or figures, is part of the original *mensonge* represented by every fictional work. If *mensonge* represents Lucien, Sartre, or both ambiguously, this does not necessarily contradict Sartre's theory; the creative process presumes the introduction and development of just such themes and figures.

One critic who finds that Sartre controls his characters in a way not unlike Mauriac is Jean-Louis Curtis in his book, *Haute Ecole* (Paris: Julliard, 1950). W. J. Harvey further maintains that in this respect Sartre reveals rather than eliminates his presence in his fictional work. He argues the following:

Indeed, I should wish to extend the argument [of Curtis] and maintain that the author's effort to eliminate himself may sometimes reveal his presence in the novel even more acutely than direct intervention. Mathieu sees his mistress Marcelle, "sitting on the edge of the bed, blankly naked and defenceless, like a great porcelain vase." Aesthetically, the comparison is only there because it anticipates his memory, a little later, of having as a child gratuitously broken a precious Chinese vase. We may accept this as natural since both image and memory belong to Mathieu's consciousness, but a little later still Marcelle thinks of Mathieu, "he really feels angry as if he had broken a vase." Sartre is scoring a point here but scoring it too obviously; attention is distracted from the characters to their creator. . . . Even more evident in *Le Sursis* . . . We cease to attend to the fiction in our quarrel wtih the author about the oversimplicity of his technique. [*Character and the Novel* (London: Chatto & Windus, 1965), pp. 168–69]

4. Critics have generally praised Sartre's ability to stay within the consciousness of his fictional characters. R. M. Albérès, for example, writes:

Ce qui serait chez un autre écrivain narration objective reste chez lui tout imprégné du goût particulier de la conscience humaine qui le vit. Nous n'assistons pas seulement aux petits événements que vit Mathieu, nous y assistons avec le même goût dans l'arrière-bouche qu'a Mathieu, avec le même relent qui est au fond de son esprit. . . . Les scènes de la rue que voit Mathieu, nous les voyons comme lui à travers le même état viscéral et coenesthésique qui est le sien. [*Jean-Paul Sartre* (Paris: Editions Universitaires, 1953), p. 122]

Stephen Ullmann attributes this particular technique to the phenomenological bent of the Sartrean art:

Everything is presented as seen and felt by the characters themselves, in a kind of perpetual and loosely constructed free indirect speech. . . . The linguistic corollary of this relativist position is an extreme form of the free indirect technique: objects and events are presented not as they are, but "phenomenologically," as experienced by a particular mind. [*Style in the French Novel* (Oxford: Basil Blackwell, 1964), p. 245]

5. *The Rhetoric of Fiction* (Chicago: U. of Chicago Press, 1961), p. 20.

W. J. Harvey has pushed this point to an extreme in the case of Sartre. He writes:

But whether successful or not, the main point still holds; the author cannot be banished from his creation. If he withholds his direct intervention, then he is still present in all the choices which determine his creative act and in all the tricks which characterize his art. It is only when the effects of either intervention or elimination are too obvious that we object. The contradiction at the heart of Sartre's literary theory becomes a paradox of creation; the more absolute the illusion of freedom, the more absolute the real, though disguised, artistic control. [p. 171]

6. For an extremely lucid presentation of this narrative mode, which is an English translation of the German *erlebte Rede*, see Dorrit Cohn, "Narrated Monologue: Definition of a Fictional Style," *Comparative Literature*, 18:2 (spring 1966), 97–112.

Mrs. Cohn defines narrated monologue grammatically as "the presentation of a character's thoughts in the third person and the tense of narration" which allows the reader to

move closer to the possibility of rendering such thoughts and feelings of a character as are not explicitly formulated in his mind. Since the figural voice is not quoted directly, as it is in the interior monologue, this technique lends itself better to the twilight realm of consciousness . . . the narrated monologue shades into internal analysis, where the author reports—no matter how unobtrusively—on the inner life of his figures, making the haziest thoughts accessible to language, translating an unorganized inner world into a communicable idiom. The narrated monologue, no less than the interior monologue, posits the existence of an inner voice with which a consciousness addresses itself; and its narrator is, in a sense, the imitator of his character's silent utterances. [P. 110]

Further, Mrs. Cohn outlines two divergent directions open to the narrated monologue: the lyric and the ironic. She cites Sartre's *L'Enfance d'un chef* as a prime example of the ironic. Although Camus's *L'Étranger* is narrated in the first rather than the third person, becoming interior monologue rather than remaining narrated monologue, I would like to suggest by my comparison that Camus's technique is not far removed from Sartre's, with the exception that Camus opts for the lyric there where Sartre opts for the ironic.

7. Magny denies Lucien's ability ever to speak in the first person at all. Her theory classifying all Sartre's early heroes as *tricheurs*, includes Lucien as a *tricheur de dixième zone*, or, in Sartre's words, as a "salaud." As such, she finds that he does not have an experience authentic enough to communicate in the first person, and that Sartre must present such "salauds" in the third person so that their bad faith, or *tricherie*, becomes evident. Pp. 124–32.

It is precisely because Lucien is not entirely a "salaud," because Sartre presents him as simultaneously antipathetic and sympathetic, as "salaud" and "not-salaud," that is, from a double point of view, that Lucien can and does speak in the first person. As Lucien develops more and more definitively into a "salaud," it is true that his first person appears less and less frequently. Sartre finds substitutes for the "je" form, however, which are enumerated later in this chapter.

8. This is Sartre's theory about time in the novel expressed here succinctly by Pouillon in "Règles du je," *Les Temps modernes,* 12:134 (April 1957), 1594.

9. Philip Thody, while finding this "perhaps the best ending of any of Sartre's short stories," believes this is so precisely because Sartre breaks away from Lucien's point of view. He compares Lucien to Daniel of *L'Age de raison* in this respect: "In both cases the reader is suddenly taken from inside the character's mind to a position where he contemplates him from outside. It is the contrast between what the character thinks he is—a leader among Frenchmen, an avenging archangel—and his objective reality—a delicate adolescent, an old queen carrying a box of sweets—which provides the humour. In both cases, the effect is one which Sartre obtains by suddenly breaking his own rules, and seeing his character from a detached viewpoint of the traditional novelist." *Jean-Paul Sartre: A Literary and Political Study* (London: Hamilton, 1960), pp. 35, 49.

Oleg Koefoed had earlier pointed to this ending as one at which "le fou rire se déchaîne." He finds that the genius of this story lies in Sartre's handling of just such "fierce" humor throughout. "L'Oeuvre littéraire de Sartre," *Orbis Litterarum,* VI (1948), 272.

10. There has been some confusion among critics as to just how sympathetically Sartre portrays Lucien. Madeleine Smith finds that Sartre retains sympathy for Lucien and expects the reader to do likewise. "The author sees to it that some shred of reader-sympathy is left for his young protagonist. This is his creature; and besides, he has been showing Lucien to us as a victim, not as a villain." "The Making of a Leader," *Yale French Studies No. 1* (spring-summer, 1948), p. 82.

Other critics find that Lucien seems to be a sympathetic character because he illustrates some of Sartre's favorite themes, but that he never completely vindicates himself. "Up to his unfortunate decision, however, Lucien illustrates in miniature a number of Sartre's ideas on the nature of the human mind, and seems to be on the point of acquiring Roquentin's lucidity." Thody, p. 33.

Magny groups Lucien with other Sartrean "salauds" presented initially in a sympathetic light but who eventually slide into the collective consciousness and drag the reader with them. "Sartre nous permet de sympathiser juste assez avec Lucien pour que sa désagrégation et son reniement final nous atteignent" (p. 141). Sartre may be said to condemn Lucien wholeheartedly in the light of his later polemic on the anti-Semite: *Réflexions sur la question juive*. Sartre's antipathy toward and condemnation of Lucien from the very beginning become more evident upon each rereading of *L'Enfance d'un chef*.

11. Fredric Jameson's syntactical analysis of Sartre's style further elucidates such climactic moments.

> The normal connection in [Sartre's] special world is not the period at all but the comma. . . . When the period is frequently used in a paragraph, the past definite is called into play and the effect is that of a jerky moving forward in time. . . . This abnormal strength of the period accounts for the very frequent use of the semicolon. [*Sartre: The Origins of a Style* (New Haven: Yale University Press, 1961), pp. 42–43]

12. This is an excellent example of Magny's second point about Sartre's use of the imperfect and the *passé simple* tenses in *L'Enfance d'un chef*. (See n. 15.) Here, as in an example Magny cites to illustrate her point, we can note in Sartre's verb tâta, "la façon dont le passé simple vient mettre le point final à la rêverie de Lucien et le rendre à la réalité" (p. 139).

13. The term "objective correlative," introduced by T. S. Eliot, has been applied to objects which support or reinforce, thus are the "correlative" of, certain emotional states an author might wish to convey. In some instances in recent fiction, the object might go so far as to incorporate or signify the emotional state. Sartre, as well as Camus and Robbe-Grillet, makes extensive use of this technique.

In *L'Enfance d'un chef*, Lucien's cane, used to whip the nettles while screaming, "J'aime ma maman, j'aime ma maman" (p. 154), and which later reappears as a symbol of his commitment to the camelots (p. 229), might be considered a stage-prop correlative of Lucien's sentiment.

More interesting in this respect, however, are Sartre's descriptions which are distorted by Lucien's perspective, so that the description itself becomes a correlative of his emotion. In the example already cited, a tunnel concretely materializes in Lucien's imagination as the forgotten memory, and comes to signify his fear as well. This tunnel is most obviously a Freudian symbol, but it also characterizes Lucien's distorting perspective as Sartre represents it.

The following description will demonstrate Sartre's distorting perspective through the eyes of Lucien as a child in order to recapture his childhood experience of time. This same descriptive technique was exploited by Joyce in the first pages of his *Portrait of the Artist* in the attempt to recapture Stephen Dedalus's childish sensibility.

"Lucien pensa à une bicyclette que son papa devait lui acheter, il entendit le sifflement d'une locomotive, et puis, tout d'un coup, la bonne entra et tira les rideaux, il était huit heures du matin." [P. 158]

Lucien's emotion again distorts perspective in the following descriptive passage:

"Ça n'était pas agréable; les bergers avaient sauté en arrière, il semblait à Lucien qu'il les regardait par le gros bout d'une lorgnette." [P. 171]

The shepherds do not actually jump backwards; they do so only through the imposition of Lucien's distorting point of view in this episode. The shepherds are figures printed on the wallpaper of Lucien's room at which he is staring at the precise moment he "awakens" from his long somnolent state.

Later, objective description again finds its origins in Lucien's dizziness at a moment of climactic emotion. At the moment Lucien realizes why Bergère has befriended him, rather than an objective statement such as, "Lucien became dizzy with fear," Sartre writes the following:

"Et les losanges de la tapisserie se mirent à tourner pendant que l'étouffante odeur d'eau de Cologne le saisissait à la gorge." [P. 195]

Subsequently New Novelists exploit this distorting perspective through description.

Stephen Ullmann's following comment on Sartre's imagery obtains here: "Most of the images occur in internal monologues, in Sartre's particular brand of free indirect style. He is trying to record the associations arising spontaneously in the minds of his characters; the thoughts are theirs, not his own. It is not suggested that the free indirect method affords an easy alibi for every kind of licence, but it is certainly relevant to the interpretation of Sartre's imagery" (p. 259).

14. For an exposition of all Sartre's and Robbe-Grillet's protagonists as "psychotic" precisely because of experiences such as Lucien's dissociation here, cf. Dennis Porter, "Sartre, Robbe-Grillet, and the psychotic hero," *Modern Fiction Studies,* 16:1 (spring 1970).

15. Magny attributes this effect to Sartre's particular, and novel, use of the imperfect tense. Sartre's predominant imperfect tense makes Lucien's story seem to take place in a distant past rather than in a present. Lucien's actions as well as his thoughts are reduced to a reverie, a fantasy, or a day-dream. To Magny, there is no difference, hence no esthetic tension, between Lucien's real experiences and his fancied experiences.

She maintains that Sartre couples the traditional use of the imperfect with the "Flaubertian" use of the imperfect, which results in a novel effect. Describing a *new* experience for Lucien in the imperfect, that is, makes the experience seem to have happened before. Her two main points and resulting conclusions are the following:

(1) Ces actions ou impressions, pourtant nouvelles pour le héros, du fait qu'elles soient racontées à l'imparfait, semblent répéter en écho une infinité d'actions analogues qui les auraient précédées, comme en un cauchemar paramnésique, où tout est *déjà* arrivé mille fois. En même temps l'imparfait a un autre usage: (2) il fait apparaître la vie pourtant réelle, du personnage, comme quelque chose à quoi il ne participe pas, qui se déroule pour ainsi dire hors de lui,—une mélopée qu'il se chantonnerait à mi-voix en lui-même, mais qui concerne quelqu'un d'autre. Il est alors le temps du *day-dream,* du rêve les yeux ouverts. . . .

Une leçon très subtile se dégage de cet artifice de style: en employant des moyens identiques pour exprimer deux choses en apparence différentes: action stéréotypée, rêverie imprécise, Sartre nous fait sentir que la vie imaginaire n'est pas moins sclérosée que l'existence "officielle," à la manière des salauds. Ni l'une ni l'autre ne constituent un affranchissement véritable, une conquête de la liberté. [Pp. 138–39]

Mme Magny's description of Sartre's use of the "imperfect" here sounds convincingly like a precise description of Robbe-Grillet's *Dans le Labyrinthe.* As yet unaware of the New Novel, Mme Magny's perspicacious analysis of Sartre's "imperfect" has proved through time to be particularly relevant and exact.

16. The paradox and, at the same time, the genius of Sartre's role between his protagonist and his readers is provocatively expressed by Jacques Ehrmann in his article, "Of Rats and Men: Notes on the Prefaces," *Yale French Studies No. 30.*

"He" denounces us to ourselves, "we" in turn become victims.

Between the work and the reader, the "him" and the "us," Sartre, himself sundered, plies to and fro. Sundered because as a reader he knows how to recognize what separates him from the work; identifying himself with the work, he sees what separates him from the public.

He is the victim and the executioner of the work he offers. This work, the work of a victim, is also the work of our victim who yet is able to judge us and so win his victory.

17. Most critics agree with Harvey, who is otherwise a hostile critic, that "it is precisely this emphasis on the reader's activity that is the valuable element in Sartre's theory" (p. 164).

Jameson makes this point more explicit:

The reader is built into the style, the deliberate imperfection of the sentences requires the corrections his mind will perform on them to make them express reality. The distance between the

sentence and its meaning must be filled with the subjectivity of
the reader himself just as in the form the distance between
consciousness and facticity drew him into complicity, and made
him assume and live that facticity instead of abolishing it
through some unique organizational vision. [P. 201]

## Chapter 3

1. Most critics accepted Camus's present moment as existentially "complete and sufficient unto itself," after Sartre's early discovery 1) that in *L'Étranger* "Seul le présent compte, le concret,"
and 2) that Camus uses the perfect tense in his book as a "succession
de présents inertes." "l'Explication de *L'Étranger*," *Situations I*
(Paris: Gallimard, 1947).

Subsequent critics, such as J. Cruickshank, linked Camus's
present moment to the "divorce" between Meursault and society
described as the "absurd" in *Le Mythe de Sisyphe. Albert Camus and
the Literature of Revolt* (London: Oxford U. P., 1959).

Others, like C. Gadourek, adopted Meursault's perspective in
order to show that even from his own point of view, Meursault feels
enclosed in an eternal present when he relates, "C'était sans cesse
le même jour qui déferlait dans ma cellule." *Les Innocents et les
Coupables* (La Haye: Mouton, 1963), p. 64.

There has been much critical speculation based on this precise
combination of the first person with the *passé composé* in *L'Étranger*,
which holds it responsible for the detached tone or "indifférence" or
"absurdity" of Meursault. Some of the more important inquiries into
this aspect of *L'Étranger* are the following:

M. G. Barrier, *L'Art du récit dans* L'Étranger *d'Albert Camus* (Paris:
Nizet, 1962).

B. T. Fitch, *Narrateur et narration dans* L'Étranger *d'Albert Camus*
(Paris: Lettres Modernes, Minard, 1960, 2d ed., 1968).

J.-C. Pariente, "L'Étranger et son double," *Revue des lettres modernes*, 170–74, *Autour de* L'Étranger, 1968, 53–80.

André Abbou, "Les paradoxes du discours dans *L'Étranger:* De la
parole directe à l'écriture inverse," *Revue des lettres modernes*,
212–16, *Langue et Langages*, 1969, 35–76.

2. Sartre, "L'Explication de *L'Étranger*," pp. 117–18. For an
opposite analysis, see Cruickshank, who finds Camus's prose "verb-
centered" rather than "noun-centered," and considers it evidence of
the "absurd" experience. P. 161.

It might be added that this emphasis upon nouns rather than
upon verbs results on a larger scale in a series of static scenes, or
*tableaux,* as the compound effect of *L'Étranger*, which concomitantly
deemphasizes its kinetic linear development of plot. The concrete
static, i.e., of what "is," dominates the vibrant kinetic force of "becoming" to such an extent in *L'Étranger* that it might be classified a
spatial work in accordance with Frank's definition of that form. 221–
41, 433–56, 643–54.

Such *tableaux* make of *L'Étranger* a "pictorial book," which
lends itself by definition to a study of point of view in the sense
Lubbock originally defined it.

3. Sartre, "L'Explication de *L'Étranger*," p. 120.

4. *Narrateur et narration dans* L'Étranger *d'Albert Camus*, 2d ed., rev. and aug. (Paris: Minard, 1968), p. 10.

5. *Le Sentiment de l'étrangeté chez Malraux, Sartre, Camus et Simone de Beauvoir*, Bibliothèque des Lettres Modernes (Paris: Minard, 1964), p. 193.

6. Abbou.

7. Page references, hereafter following quotations, are to the Pléiade edition of *L'Étranger*, 1962.

8. For a more complete account of Camus's two styles, which differs somewhat from the one given here, see Stephen Ullmann, "The Two Styles of Camus," *The Image in the Modern French Novel* (Oxford: Blackwell, 1963), pp. 239–99.

9. After Sartre first contended that Camus's *passé composé* constitutes in reality a present, subsequent critics justified Camus's *passé composé* as some sort of modified perfect tense in contradistinction to the preterite. Generally, most agreed with Cruickshank that "the preterite is the tense of *lived* experience whereas the perfect is the tense of *living* experience. . . . [The use of the perfect tense in *L'Étranger*] gives to events an actuality which virtually makes a composite present out of the author's presentation of time and time as experienced by the reader" (pp. 159–60).

Champigny found Camus's use of the *passé composé* technically responsible for the ambiguity in Meursault's perspective between his *moi présent* and his *moi passé* which permits Camus to place himself simultaneously in the first person of both. *Sur un héros païen* (Paris: Gallimard, 1959), p. 147.

For Barrier, the *passé composé* of *L'Étranger* lent atmosphere or dramatic relief to each action; it was a question of tone rather than of occurrence. Barrier discovered, in addition, five verbs in the *passé simple* in *L'Étranger* which he properly labelled "inadvertences" of Camus. They are: "frappa, donna" on p. 25, "passèrent" on p. 35, "arrivèrent" on p. 37, and "dura" on p. 100 of the NRF edition of *L'Étranger*. Pp. 6–19.

10. Fitch believes that the first sentence of the book alone determines the present mode for the remainder of *L'Étranger*. *Narrateur et narration*, p. 26.

Barrier believes that the beginning of each chapter establishes a "climate," or installs the reader in the present while it is being lived, after which Camus can forget these beginnings of each chapter. He finds that signs of the present instant hide fictional distance ("recul romanesque") which exists nevertheless. Camus wished to plunge the reader into Meursault's life *in medias res*, as it were, by reducing the temporal distance between the narrator and what is narrated. Pp. 26–28.

Cruickshank finds that the *passé composé* occasions the extention of the past into the present, thus adding to the events of *L'Étranger* "a quality of continuation from their occurrence up to the moment of their narration by Meursault" (p. 161).

11. Consistent perhaps with Camus's wish to structure first and

last chapters similarly, Gadourek discovers Camus's intention to structure the two parts similarly in his unpublished notebooks, but fails to indicate her precise source. P. 87.

12. The first critic to divide *L'Étranger* into three parts was Carl A. Viggiani, "Camus's 'L'Étranger," *PMLA*, 71:5 (December 1956), 866.

13. Fitch has the impression that Meursault-the-narrator is a separate person from Meursault-the-hero, and that from the beginning the reader is established in the mind of the former. Meursault-the-narrator, however, identifies totally with his past experiences throughout his narration in such a way that the reader is not at all conscious of his presence as the narrator. *Narrateur et narration*, p. 23.

According to Champigny, on the contrary, it is insofar as Meursault is established as the narrator from the beginning that he can appear as a stranger. *Sur un héros païen*, p. 26.

14. Champigny senses also that Meursault pleads his case constantly from beginning to end. He indicates the precise moment at which he believes the reader becomes aware of it: "Or, au moment où débute la seconde partie, au moment où Meursault est interrogé par le juge d'instruction, le lecteur se rend compte que le récit qu'il a lu jusqu'à présent équivaut aux déclarations de Meursault devant ses juges" (p. 35).

15. Among the critics who have established time schemes for *L'Étranger*, three of the most exact are those of Fitch, (*Narrateur et narration*, pp. 24–25), Gadourek (pp. 69–72), and Pariente. The first two schemas represent the opposing opinions most prevalent among contemporary critics. Fitch believes that no explanation could justify Meursault if the events of his narrative were narrated as they occurred. There is a constant temporal hiatus between narrator and events, rather, because "Le présent du narrateur se situe au même moment pendant toute la durée du roman, c'est-à-dire vers la fin, au début de son dernier chapitre" (p. 29). The entire story is told in retrospect, according to Fitch and Champigny.

Gadourek, on the other hand, painstakingly establishes a temporal schema more consonant with that of the majority of critics and with my own outline. She distinguishes seven moments at which Meursault recapitulates Part 1, roughly equivalent to the chapters of that part, and four moments in Part 2 during which recapitulation occurs. Whereas Meursault recalls recent past events approximately every two days in Part 1, he summarizes longer spans of time in Part 2 or describes events of capital importance such as the murder of the Arab or the visit of the priest, according to Gadourek's outline. For comparison, her time scheme is related to my own in parentheses as follows:

*Part 1*

| 1. Chapter 1 | telegram received Thurs. AM | *(Thurs., Fri.)* |
| 2. Chapter 2 | wake and funeral recalled Sat. AM | *(Sat.)* |
| 3. Chapter 3 | weekend with Marie recalled Mon. AM | *(Mon.)* |
| 4. | day at office recalled Mon. PM | |
| 5. Chapter 4 | weekend recalled Sun. PM | *(Sun.)* |
| 6. Chapter 5 | events recalled a weekday Raymond and Salamano recalled Sun. PM | *(sometime after the murder)* |

*Part 2*

| 1. Chapter 6 | murder of Arab recalled second week of prison | *(same as above)* |
| 2. Chapters 1 & 2 | prison life recalled after 11 months | *(after one year)* |
| 3. Chapters 3 & 4 | trial recalled after priest's visit | |
| 4. Chapter 4 | Meursault's personal justification recalled at daybreak | *(day of Meursault's death)* |

By plotting the chronology of *L'Étranger* on both its "temporal indicators" and its verbal tense, Pariente concludes as above that Part 1 of *L'Étranger* must have been written at five different times as if noted in a diary by Meursault. Pariente's interpretation of Part 1, chapters 5 & 6, and of Part 2 differs from previous critics' in supposing Meursault wrote them all at one sitting, in retrospect, as if they were to compose a novel of his life. Knowing himself to be different from the murderer society had tried and condemned him for, and knowing that he had to die, forced Meursault to make the supreme effort at defining himself this second part of *L'Étranger* represents. Meursault's early "diary" becomes a "novel" or a "diary disguised as a novel" according to M. Pariente's interpretation, and so multiplies the ambiguities inherent in such an understanding of *L'Étranger*. Genial as M. Pariente's analysis is, it is a bit difficult to follow his struggles in interpreting Part 2 since he does not realize that it proceeds topically rather than chronologically and treats it by the same analytical method applied to Part 1.

16. Champigny, *Le Genre romanesque,* p. 107.

17. This change in Camus's manuscript is indicated in the Pléiade edition of *L'Étranger,* n. 2 under p. 1206, on page 1919.

18. See Camus's divisions of Part 2 in the Pléiade notes to *L'Étranger,* reference to page 1167 of the text, p. 1916.

19. Grevisse, *Le Bon Usage, grammaire française* (Gembloux, Belgique: Duculot, 1959), p. 1050, Rem. 1.

20. Ibid., p. 632.

21. This is in accord with Camus's intention of creating a character who answers questions, but who never, or rarely, asks them. See the Pléiade edition of *L'Étranger* for Camus's intention expressed in a letter to A.J.T., p 1923.

22. In this scene Barrier finds that Camus screams louder than Meursault at the priest. P. 80.

23. As has been noted, the moment of this "present" differs with different critics. Fitch believes that the present of the narrator is situated at the beginning of the last chapter throughout the book. *Le Sentiment de l'étrangeté*, p. 198. Champigny believes that the present of the narrator is placed at the end of the story, after Meursault's scene with the priest. *Sur un héros païen*, p. 197. Most other critics agree with Gadourek that there are several presents which must be plotted by careful scrutiny of the text. Pp. 69–72.

It is this "série de présents successifs" which constitutes for Pariente the true originality of Camus's technique, and which he asserts Camus must have applied quite deliberately. P. 62.

24. Cruickshank, p. 161.

25. Lubbock, pp. 258–64.

The long-standing trend among American academics more recently adopted by French critics, is to analyze a novel by separating each of the several "voices" included in a single point of view. Friedman, for example, became a self-styled Darwinian literary critic classifying all possible categories of point of view. Pp. 1160–1184. His categories have frequently been applied in recent years to French New Novels by various American academics.

The only contemporary critic who pleads for a return to Lubbock's original notion of *including* the author's voice through *erlebte Rede* or *discours indirect libre* to my knowledge is Cohn.

See also Fitch, "Aspects de l'emploi du discours indirect libre dans *L'Étranger*," *Revue des lettres modernes, Autour de L'Étranger* 1, 1968.

26. *Narrateur et narration*, 2d ed., 1968, pp. 38–43.

27. Contrary to this argument, many critics agree with Fitch that the reader's complicity with Meursault begins at this point. Rather than naïveté written into the character of Meursault by Camus, Fitch accepts Meursault's words as good faith in this scene. For the first time Meursault becomes aware that others think he is guilty and a criminal, and he subsequently assumes this identity in spite of himself, according to Fitch's interpretation. *Sentiment de l'étrangeté*, p. 205.

Fitch and Gadourek believe that Meursault is a sensitive character with whom Camus is in sympathy throughout, but with whom the reader begins to sympathize only in Part 2. Champigny and Cruickshank, on the contrary, find that Camus invites the detachment of the reader's sympathy in Part 1, and then tries to justify his hero in Part 2.

In his controversial article on *L'Étranger* reexamined in the light of *La Chute*, René Girard goes a step further in claiming that Camus himself was duped by Meursault, who serves, in fact, as "an artificial bridge between the solipsist and ordinary mortals." Camus's

Stranger Retried," *PMLA*, 79:5 (December 1964), 527.

28. Fitch, "Aspects de l'emploi de discours indirect libre dans *L'Étranger*," 88ff.

29. Ibid., 87.

30. Fitch, *Narrateur et narration*, p. 45.

31. Sartre. *"L'Explication de L'Étranger*," p. 144.

32. In her American edition of *L'Étranger*, Germaine Brée interprets this image as a "kind of modulation into the key of Part 2." *L'Étranger* (N.Y.: Appleton-Century-Crofts, 1955), p. 80.

33. But this last sentence does not weaken Camus's message as a moralist. Undoubtedly Camus wanted and intended Meursault to be a Christ figure (cf. letter from Camus in the Brée edition of *L'Étranger*), but he is using the shock afforded by this last sentence to force us to accept Meursault's martyrdom with too heavy a hand.

34. It is important to specify here that "cette dualité, ou ambiguité, dans la perspective n'apparaît pas comme duplicité." Champigny, *Sur un héros païen*, p. 148.

35. Lubbock, pp. 251–64.

36. Pariente, 63.

## Chapter 4

1. Appropriately enough, Hazel E. Barnes sees Meursault's relationship to his narrative and to Camus in exactly the same terms as those advanced here concerning the narrator's relationship to his narrative and to Robbe-Grillet. Miss Barnes writes: "Meursault's narrative is aesthetic, bearing the same relation to him as an imagining consciousness that the novel bears to Camus." "Modes of Aesthetic Consciousness in Fiction," *Bucknell Review*, 2:1 (March 1964), 85.

Jean Bloch-Michel claims that the author thus integrates himself inextricably within his novel rather than distancing himself from it. He maintains that this tendency has been inherited from Céline's narrators who speak in soliloquies rather than in interior monologues.

2. Whereas most critics accept the doctor as narrator of the soldier's story on the strength of the two personal pronouns at the end, one critic, at least, concludes that the doctor cannot be the narrator because of his distinct style of expression. This critic splits the single doctor-narrator into two separate fictional characters. James Lethcoe, "The Structure of Robbe-Grillet's Labyrinth," *French Review* 38 (1965), 497–506.

Olga Bernal tends also to split the first-person narrator into two:

Le point de vue de ce roman est particulièrement intéressant parce qu'il pose le problème du rapport entre l'écrivain et le roman. . . . Il y a donc expérience de "labyrinthe" en ce qui concerne le point de vue narratif. Le "je" narrateur devient un "on" narrateur, une voix anonyme. [Pp. 172–73]

Two critics agree with me that point of view remains double, ambiguously delineated between the first-person narrator and the

third-person soldier. The first, Christine Brooke-Rose, elaborates
the ambiguity of Robbe-Grillet's narrator:

Ce narrateur est donc plus proche de l'auteur omniscient traditionnel, quoi qu'il n'intervienne pas directement, bien entendu,
mais nous verrons qu'il ne représente pas vraiment un auteur
omniscient mais plutôt le soldat perdu dans un vide atemporel,
qui guide et situe le "je" de la narration et dont le récit est
constamment enrichi; en une sorte de contrepoint, par les
remarques d'un observateur implicite qui est peut-être le narrateur à la première personne ou le soldat lui-même. ["L'Imagination baroque de Robbe-Grillet," in J. H. Mathews (ed.), *Un
nouveau Roman? Recherches et tradition, Revue des Lettres
modernes,* 1964, p. 137]

Second, Morrissette believes that Robbe-Grillet's double point of
view has an effect of simultaneity on the reader:

On se heurte tout de suite au problème soulevé par le mode
narratif, c'est-à-dire le point de vue selon lequel le lecteur est
censé "voir" le texte. . . . Tout se passe donc comme si la surface
du texte était une "surface mitoyenne" (L'expression est de
Jacques-Bernard Brunius) de l'objectif (ce que voit et imagine le
soldat) et du subjectif (ce que pense et invente le narrateur). Au
cours de cette symbiose, le texte est tour à tour attiré du côté
du soldat (à qui le narrateur voudrait qu'il s'attache) et du côté
du narrateur (on le sent à l'angoisse évidente du récitant). . . .
On éprouve simultanément l'angoisse du soldat qui se perd dans
son dédale et celle de son créateur qui le façonne et le regarde
évoluer. [*Les Romans de Robbe-Grillet* (Paris: Editions de
Minuit, 1964), pp. 158–80]

One of the most unusual interpretations of *Dans le Labyrinthe* is
the psychoanalytical one made by Didier Anzieu, who holds that all
Robbe-Grillet's work stems from the mind of an obsessive neurotic.
His comment upon Robbe-Grillet's use of the first and third persons,
while confirming his thesis, offers an interesting insight into the
author's unconscious motives for creating this particular kind of
double perspective in *Dans le Labyrinthe:*

Le monde extérieur est donc présenté à la première personne,
c'est le monde vécu par un sujet humain. Mais le sujet humain
est décrit à la troisième personne: il est objet pour le narrateur.
Là réside un nouveau dédoublement, et un nouvel isolement.
L'obsessionnel n'habite pas ce qu'il fait ou ce qu'il ressent: il se
regarde le faire ou le ressentir. Le monde qu'il habite, il l'habite
à la troisième personne. ["Le Discours de l'obsessionnel dans
les romans de Robbe-Grillet," *Les Temps modernes,* 233 (October 1965), 629]

3. Genette reasons as follows:

Le reflet, on le sait, est une forme affaiblie du *double,* qui est un compromis de *même* et *d'autre:* un *même* reproduit, donc aliéné. Forme encore atténuée de cette aliénation du *même,* la *ressemblance,* par où l'altérité mime l'identité, ou *l'altération,* par où l'identité suggère une altérité. [P. 296]

4. It is perhaps superfluous to reiterate here the role of objects and of T. S. Eliot's notion of objective correlative as found in the preceding works of Sartre and Camus. (Cf. ch. 2, n. 13.) In view of the preponderance of objects in Robbe-Grillet's works, however, and of his decided predilection for Eliot's objective correlative, it seems pertinent to note the following. Of the many critics who have commented on the role of objects in the work of Robbe-Grillet, not all have seen them as expressions of an internal consciousness as is suggested here, and even fewer, if any, have suggested that Robbe-Grillet's use (and abuse) of objects carries on a tradition well established in the works of Sartre and Camus. Bernal, however, has allied introspection with perception, memory, and imagination as I have. She writes: "Dans le roman de Robbe-Grillet, il n'y a pas d'introspection qui se passe d'images concrètes, il n'y a que la matérialité de la conscience. Souvenir, image imaginée, perception, rêve, tout y est forme visible" (p. 170).

Brooke-Rose emphasizes the powerful effect such a method has on the reader; the reader is forced to live the novel from the internal perspective of the hero, however feverish or confused his perspective may be:

Dans ce roman, il nous est donc donné de voir, à la manière du créateur, les mêmes objets dans divers cadres temporels, quoique avec le maximum d'instantanéité promis par le langage (qui prend du temps) C'est là une situation trés baroque dans laquelle tout objet peut être plusieurs choses à la fois, ou vu simultanément suivant deux ou trois perspectives différentes. Ce résultat est ici atteint grâce à l'analogue et à la juxtaposition *intérieure* au présent (en liaison avec des auxiliaires spatiaux et temporels tels que *maintenant, dehors,* etc.) plutôt qu'à l'aide de métaphores, de paradoxes explicites ou d'autres techniques spécifiquement baroques. Mais cette méthode joue constamment un rôle structurel, nous *contraignant à vivre* de l'intérieur le temps narratif de l'auteur—temps qui est lui-même assimilé aux processus étranges qui se déroulent dans l'esprit du protagoniste—et non à le vivre de l'extérieur sans renoncer à nos propres coordonnées temporelles.

Ce premier aspect de la double ambiguité est considérablement renforcé par le second, à savoir le choix comme personnage central ou sujet de l'action d'un esprit confus qui, en raison de son état percevra sans doute le monde de manière insolite parce que a-focale. [P. 147]

Morrissette first applied the term "objective correlative" to Robbe-Grillet's work, finding that objects in it serve as emotional correlatives. For this insight, he received Robbe-Grillet's blessing:

Vous m'avez sauvé du symbolisme en inventant la "corrélation objective." Bien entendu, je n'avais point inventé le "corrélatif objectif," mais je l'avais en effet proposé (1958—*French Review* et 1959—*Critique*) pour expliquer le fonctionnement des objets dans des romans comme *Le Voyeur* et *La Jalousie* sans faire appel au symbolisme proprement dit. [*Les Romans de Robbe-Grillet,* p. 29]

5. See the meticulous restoration of this chronological sequence on a triple plane by Lethcoe, 507.

6. Barnes has discussed at length how the personal vision of Robbe-Grillet's characters informs his works. Without using the term "objective correlative," her discussion of emotion conveyed by the object in Robbe-Grillet's works describes the kind of objective correlative found there. She writes: "There is no unattached emotion, as it were; it is almost as though emotions were *in* the objects and moved as the perceiver shifted his outward or inward gaze." "The Ins and Outs of Alain Robbe-Grillet," *Chicago Review* 15:3 (winter–spring, 1962), 36.

Speaking of *La Jalousie* elsewhere, she writes: "I know of no novel which so successfully allows the reader to experience the temporal and spatial sense of a subjectivity which is not his own." Still, she finds that *L'Année dernière à Marienbad* "conveys the more nearly total experience for the reason that the camera includes within the imagined scene the character's self-image." These remarks offer a clue as to what Robbe-Grillet is getting at in *Dans le Labyrinthe* by making the soldier a sort of "self-image" of the narrator. "Modes of Aesthetic Consciousness," 85, 86.

Bernal, without denying the subjective aspect of Robbe-Grillet's novel, finds that its particular quality is to know its own limitations:

Cette non-distinction entre les images imaginées et les formes perçues dans le monde extérieur ne veut nullement dire confusion des deux modes d'être. . . . Ce vers quoi tend son roman, c'est de conférer un statut de plein droit à la réalité créée par la conscience, par la vision d'un homme. Mais la vision d'un homme particulier sera relative à sa situation, à ses obsessions *à lui*. . . . Il s'agit donc d'une subjectivité qui ne s'ignore pas. Et là est le caractère nouveau de cette subjectivité . . . le roman de Robbe-Grillet devient un roman relatif et non plus un roman subjectif.

La nature relative du roman impose des limites à la conscience individuelle, lui rappelle qu'elle crée sa propre vision du monde, mais que le monde n'est pas pour autant le reflet de cette vision. [Pp. 183–84]

7. Champigny, *Le Genre romanesque*, p. 50.

8. Page references, hereafter following quotations, are to Alain Robbe-Grillet, *Dans le Labyrinthe* (Paris: Éditions de Minuit, 1959). This first sentence of the *Labyrinthe*, as pointed out by Roland Barthes, is a perfect example of J. Austin's concept of the "performative" mode of discourse which accompishes an action (ex.: "I give you my word") in contradistinction to the "constative" mode which merely designates an action ("I give you my briefcase"). According to this view, Robbe-Grillet's words literally accomplish the "action" of the novel, here the "action" of establishing the narrator in the room at the moment of reading the sentence.

9. At the very end of the novel, the following passage reiterates the beginning description, with the single difference that it pertains to rain rather than to sun or snow: "Dehors il pleut. Dehors on marche sous la pluie en courbant la tête, s'abritant les yeux d'une main tout en regardant quand même devant soi, à quelques mètres devant soi, quelques mètres d'asphalte mouillé. Ici la pluie n'entre pas . . ." (p. 220).

10. See ch. 1, n. 35. Morrissette first mentioned the picture as center of the myth it propagates in this novel when he noted: "Il y a un centre où convergent tous les fils d'Ariane possibles: c'est le tableau" (*Les Romans de Robbe-Grillet*, p. 161).

11. Bernal has also sensed this visual aspect of Robbe-Grillet's work. She writes: "L'image visuelle est si naturelle chez Robbe-Grillet que même une conversation entre deux personnages se transforme aussitôt en ce qu'il appelle un *échange de vues* et, ici, l'expression reprend tout son sens littéral" (p. 177).

Her following remark suggests Robbe-Grillet's heritage from the Camus of *L'Étranger* where "je regarde" equals in a similar way "je comprends." "En matière ontologique, 'je regarde' équivaut à 'je pense'. . . . Les rapports entre les personnages sont essentiellement de regard à regard" (p. 195).

Mme Bernal finally augments Robbe-Grillet's acute sense of the visual into a metaphysical crisis in this work:

*Dans le Labyrinthe* est en quelque sorte une crise du regard. . .

C'est dans cette incapacité de regard à devenir obsession, à se dépasser ainsi vers autre chose que soi-même, que réside la portée métaphysique du regard dans le *Labyrinthe*.

L'impossibilité à dépasser la réalité purement humaine se ramène à cette absence . . . de quelque chose, d'une part essentielle à l'homme, capable de provoquer une transcendance, une croyance ou, en termes robbegrilletiens, capable de faire disparaître le creux au coeur de la réalité. . . . Dans le *Labyrinthe*, l'interrogation (de Joseph K. dans *Le Procès* de Kafka) est remplacée par le regard. Il a pour fonction d'empêcher la fuite vers le dépassement. . . . Sa fonction est de maintenir la

conscience au ras du réel, dans "l'ici et le maintenant" visible,
d'endiguer ainsi l'existence pour qu'elle ne renvoie à rien
d'autre qu'elle-même, pour que tout dépassement lui demeure
interdit. [Pp. 206-7]

For an opposing opinion, see the article of Brooke-Rose, who
finds transitions dependent upon contrast rather than upon visual
analogies: "Le changement ne procède donc pas par analogie visuelle
(positive ou négative), mais par un contraste violent qui nous fait
passer d'un lieu désert à une scène de foule" (p. 141).

12. For the two opposing opinions which consider Robbe-
Grillet's work 1) primarily cinematic, and 2) primarily literary, see
the following:

En fin de compte, les nouvelles techniques consistent surtout,
pour le roman, à s'interdire ce qui lui est possible, et à copier
des procédés, par lesquels le cinéma tente de faire ce qui ap-
paraissait d'abord comme lui étant impossible. [Bloch-Michel,
p. 102]

Les effets de Robbe-Grillet sont essentiellement littéraires.
Il ne sauraient être obtenus à l'aide d'une caméra sans recourir
à des gros plans terrifiants qui, bien entendu, permettraient aux
spectateurs "normaux" que nous sommes de nous souvenir, donc
de *ne pas* nous perdre, de *ne pas* nous assimiler au soldat, mais
de demeurer à l'extérieur. [Brooke-Rose, p. 148]

13. This interpretation is originally suggested by Lethcoe, 497–
507. After choosing the present "il neige," however, after "Il neige.
Il a neigé, il neigeait, il neige" (14), Lethcoe claims that the entire
narrative follows in the present tense. Such a contention simplifies
Robbe-Grillet's novel, and it remains the opinion of the majority of
critics, but it hardly explains those passages which do appear in past
tenses, particularly at the end of the narrative.

14. The scene on pages 107–09 of the text recalls the boy's
initial remarks to the soldier reported on pp. 42–43 and on p. 30, but
in reverse order. Since the soldier is feverish and dying, all his later
fantasy-repetitions forecast his doom by reverse action of the original
events; that is to say, by withdrawal, departure, and, in this instance
by dialogue in reverse.

Brooke-Rose agrees with me that the soldier's vision is consistently that of a dying man:

Il voit les objets avec une intense clarté mais, tandis qu'il agonise,
il éprouve le besoin de faire l'inventaire complet de la chambre,
ce qui laisse entendre que son obsession des choses—voire le
livre tout entier—se définit comme l'inventaire désespéré d'un
agonisant. [P. 148]

15. Lethcoe, 501.

16. See, for example, the following variety of interpretations of this same effect with respect to the reader:

> Le rôle qu'on attribue au lecteur n'est donc pas de croire que les personnages qu'on lui montre s'ennuient, c'est de comprendre à quel point le monde où on le transporte est celui de l'ennui. . . . Longtemps [les auteurs] s'étaient contentés de représenter l'ennui, aujourd'hui ils l'infligent. [Bloch-Michel, p. 63]

> Ces événements sont présentés *instantanément*, quoique hors de temps, étant vécus et revécus à travers le délire du soldat agonisant qui confère à toutes les données des jours précédents une sorte d'intensité onirique qui autorise à son tour la confusion des temps, et l'introduction d'un certain flou, en même temps qu'elle trouble toute notion d'identité subjective, si bien que le soldat a pu se voir de l'intérieur et revivre, tout à la fois, certains incidents ou épisodes, avec des omissions, des modifications ou des précisions nouvelles, perçus pour ainsi dire à travers le diaphragme élargi rétréci de l'imagination et de la mémoire; mais ces faits de conscience se mêlent avec une égale instantanéité à son expérience directe. Le passage au "je" de la fin ne représente qu'un nouveau déplacement télescopique, qui parachève (ou situe) le sentiment que nous avons, d'avoir *nous aussi* subi ces données telles qu'il (ou telles que *quelqu'un*) les a reconstruites, de l'extérieur. [Brooke-Rose, p. 145]

In his psychoanalytic study of Robbe-Grillet's works, Anzieu points out that the "lecteur devient l'interlocuteur du héros ou du narrateur," and that if the reader decides there is nothing to understand in these works, "le narrateur a gagné: le lecteur n'a rien vu de ce que le narrateur voulait lui dissimuler, tout en ayant égrené pour lui chaque pion nécessaire à la reconstitution du drame secret" (611, 612).

17. Sturrock, *The French New Novel* (Oxford. U. P., 1969), p. 23.

18. Sartre, "Explication de '*L'Étranger*,' " pp. 99–119.
See also Richard Howard's English translation in which the *passé composé* is consistently translated "has seen," "has walked," "has looked," rather than "saw," "walked," or "looked." The present effect in English is similar to that described by Sartre.

19. Robbe-Grillet clearly develops this use of the past tenses one step further than in *Le Voyeur*, where Genette points out that the imperfect tense signifies only the protagonist's memories from childhood, while the *passé composé* and the present signify action in the immediate past or present. He finds no consistent use of the past tense in *Dans le Labyrinthe*, however, but on the contrary signals this book as one written in the tense "le plus commode parce que le plus universel (à la fois descriptif et narratif): le présent" (p. 282).

Bernal bases her similar conclusion on Robbe-Grillet's statement about the present tense:

Ce temps grammatical du présent choisi par Robbe-Grillet, et auquel il se tient rigoureusement, est celui qui convient le mieux à la description de l'émotivité pure. "Une imagination, si elle est assez vive, est toujours au présent" (p. 16 de *L'Année dernière à Marienbad*). [*Robbe-Grillet, Le Roman de l'absence* (Paris, Gallimard, 1964), p. 187]

The entire book by Bloch-Michel, on the other hand, is based on the present tense as one which lacks all sentiment and is therefore typical of all "new novels."

20. Ben Stoltzfus has pushed interpretation of Robbe-Grillet's forms to the extreme of considering this figure a mandala which, according to Jung and to Indian philosophers, always indicates a unifying, or at least a unique and important, moment in the life of an individual. Along this same line, one could interpret the size of the boy's boots—33, 34, or 35—in relationship with the soldier's identification number—12345—and with the moment at which the soldier's comrade dies—the same moment his clock stops, 3:45—as numerological mysteries grouped around the number 3, which fundamentally denotes the solution of conflict. Could the soldier's death represent the solution of conflict? A Freudian might presume the cross-bayonet motif a phallic as well as a death symbol, with the numbers indicative of the soldier's approximate age, since he indicates to the doctor just before being shot that he is in his early thirties. A theologian might emphasize the death symbol with an eye to the lost father suggestion; the lost father, moreover, is a constant motif in Robbe-Grillet's works. The one person who has written about Robbe-Grillet from the psychoanalytical point of view does note the lost father motif: "Un trait commun aux héros de Robbe-Grillet est qu'il sont sans famille, ou, plus précisément, de père inconnu ou absent" (Anzieu, 633). His final interpretation of the soldier in the *Labyrinthe*, however, differs from all others in seeing the soldier's death as caused by his unacknowledged love for the woman. He reasons as follows: "Il est blessé à mort; il ne peut pas la posséder, mais il est mort de l'avoir désirée; c'est agonisant qu'il entre dans son lit. . . . Le noyau du drame de l'obsessionnel est que l'amour de la femme est mortel" (624).

If one considered Robbe-Grillet's forms indicative of archetypal dream patterns, or basic poetic archetypes as outlined by Bachelard, for example, the cold snow of the labyrinthine daydream could only indicate death. Bachelard's hypothesis of the labyrinth finding its source primarily in the geometrical sensibility, moreover, would indicate *Dans le Labyrinthe* as a particularly felicitous expression of Robbe-Grillet's sensibility. But Robbe-Grillet leaves all such interpretations up to his reader's sensibility, and although his literary game with forms and numbers seems arbitrary and gratuitous, it is more likely meaningful in the context of archetypal or unconscious determinants. See Gaston Bachelard, *La Terre et les rêveries du repos* (Paris: José Corti, 1948), pp. 210–60.

21. "Ces négations sont peut-être ce qui nous rapproche le plus de la technique baroque qui consiste à particulariser un objet en envisageant son contraire, bien que la négation elle-même repose ici sur une analogie" (Brooke-Rose, p. 150).

22. Genette claims that this might represent a "système peut-être spontané, d'ailleurs, car même les personnes les moins cultivées racontent leurs rêves à l'imparfait, et au présent le film ou la pièce de théâtre qu'elles viennent de voir, réservant le passé composé à la narration des événements réels" (p. 282).

23. Barnes has best discussed differences between the perceptive, the imaginative, and the emotional modes of esthetic consciousness in modern French fiction, specifically with respect to Sartre, Camus, and Robbe-Grillet. Her statements about *La Jalousie* are even more valid when applied to *Dans le Labyrinthe:*

At times the perceptions are "straight" as though seen by a camera; they offer perhaps the clearest example of imaginary perceiving which one can find in the novel. At other times both perceived and imagined objects are so distorted that we are clearly in the emotional mode despite the unemotional, almost clinical description of them.

24. Bernard Pingaud, *Dans le Labyrinthe* d'Alain Robbe-Grillet, *Les Lettres nouvelles* (October 7, 1959), 38–41.

25. Stoltzfus, p. 91.

26. Brooke-Rose points out this passage as particularly baroque: "(idée baroque s'il en fût)" (p. 132).

27. Frequently upon the first appearance of characters in the narrative, they are referred to as "personnages." Although this word can signify "persons" in a rather pejorative fashion, it more often signifies "characters" in a drama or novel. For example, see pp. 39, 99, 128, 139,, and 204 of the text.

28. This emphasis on visual, concrete, and static scenes places the *Labyrinthe* squarely in the tradition of the primarily pictorial (according to James/Lubbock) or spatial (according to Joyce/Frank) novel, as outlined in my Introduction.

29. See Stoltzfus. This marble "eye" on a different plane might best be allied to Robbe-Grillet's game with perspective, which clearly haunts him at the center of all his works.

30. Sturrock, p. 230.

31. Ibid., pp. 23–32.

32. C.G. Jung, *Mandala Symbolism*, trans. R.F.C. Hull (Princeton: Bollingen Series, 1959 & 1972), p. 4.

33. See Bachelard, n. 20; Georges Poulet, *Métamorphoses du cercle* (Paris: Plon, 1961); Enrico Garzilli, *Circles without Center* (Cambridge: Harvard U.P., 1972); and Ana María Barrenechea, *Borges the Labyrinth Maker* (N.Y.: New York U.P.).

34. Jorge Luis Borges, *Labyrinths: Selected Stories and Other Writings*, ed. D.A. Yates and J. E. Irby (N.Y.: New Directions,

1962), p. 23.

35. Ibid., p. 26.

36. Ibid., p. 27.

37. Ibid., p. 28.

38. See this painting of Jorge Federico Watts, "El Minotaure," reproduced in Emilio Carilla, "Un cuento de Borges", *Studia Philologica, Homanaje ofrecido a Dámaso Alonso*. (Madrid: ed. Gredos, 1960), vol. I, pp. 295–306.

39. Mircea Eliade, *Patterns in Comparative Religion,* trans. Rosemary Sheed (N.Y.: The World Pub. Co., Meridian Books, 1958), pp. 378–81. Although "archetypes" is understood differently by Jung and Eliade, Jung's unconscious archetypes often serve to explain Eliade's more manifest archetypes, so that in this instance with respect to the labyrinth their two concepts overlap.

40. Ibid., p. 381.

41. Ibid., p. 382.

42. Ibid., p. 385.

43. Ibid., p. 448.

# SELECT BIBLIOGRAPHY

This bibliography includes books and articles cited in this study and others directly relevant to it.

## General

Albérès, R. M. *Métamorphoses du roman*. Paris: A. Michel, 1966.

_____. *Le Roman d'aujourd'hui, 1960–1970*. Paris: A. Michel, 1970.

Bachelard, Gaston. *La Terre et les rêveries du repos*. Paris: Corti, 1948.

Barrenechea, Ana María. *Borges the Labyrinth Maker*. New York: New York University Press, 1965.

Barthes, Roland. *Le Degré zéro de l'écriture*. Paris: Seuil, 1953.

_____. *Essais critiques*. Paris: Seuil, 1964.

Bloch-Michel, Jean. *Le Présent de l'indicatif: essai sur le nouveau roman*. Paris: Gallimard, 1963.

Booth, Wayne C. *The Rhetoric of Fiction*. Chicago: University of Chicago Press, 1961.

Borges, Jorge Luis. *Labyrinths: Selected Stories and Other Writings,* ed. Yates and Irby. New York: New Directions, 1962.

Butor, Michel. *Répertoire I*. Paris: Gallimard, 1960.

_____. *Répertoire II*. Paris: Gallimard, 1964.

Carilla, Emilio. "Un cuento de Borges," *Studia Philologica: Homanaje ofrecido a Dámaso Alonso*. Madrid: Editiones Gredos, 1960.

Champigny, Robert. *Le Genre romanesque*. Monte-Carlo: Editions Regain, 1963.

_____. *Pour une esthétique de l'essai, analyses critiques (Breton, Sartre, Robbe-Grillet)*. Paris: Minard, Lettres Modernes, 1967.

Curtis, Jean-Louis. *Haute Ecole*. Paris: Julliard, 1950.

Eliade, Mircea. *Patterns in Comparative Religion,* trans. R. Sheed. New York: Meridian Books, 1958.

Falk, Eugene H. *Types of Thematic Structure: The Nature and Function of Motifs in Gide, Camus and Sartre*. Chicago University Press, 1967.

Frank, Joseph. "Spatial Form in Modern Literature." *Sewanee Review,* 52 (1945), 221–41, 435–56, 643–53.

Friedman, Norman. "Point of View in Fiction: The Development of a Critical Concept." *PMLA*, 70 (December 1955), 1160–84.

Frohock, Wilbur. *Style and Temper: Studies in French Fiction 1925–1960*. Cambridge: Harvard University Press, 1967.

Genette, Girard. *Figures*. Paris: Seuil, 1966.

_____. *Figures II*. Paris: Seuil, 1969.

Grevisse, Maurice. *Le Bon Usage*. Gembloux, Belgique: J. Duculot, 1959.

Grossvogel, David I. *Limits of the Novel: Evaluations of a Form from Chaucer to Robbe-Grillet*. Ithaca, New York: Cornell University Press, 1968.

Harvey, W. J. *Character and the Novel*. London: Chatto and Windus, 1965.

Heath, Stephen. *The Nouveau Roman*. Philadelphia: Temple University Press, 1972.

Huizinga, Johan. *Homo Ludens*. Boston: Beacon Press, 1950.

Jung, C. G. *Mandala Symbolism*, trans. R. F. C. Hull. Princeton: Bollingen Series, 1959–1972.

Lawall, Sarah. *Critics of Consciousness: The Existential Structures of Literature*. Cambridge: Harvard University Press, 1968.

Lubbock, Percy. *The Craft of Fiction*. New York: The Viking Press, 1957.

Magny, Claude-Edmonde. *Les Sandales d'Empédocle*. Neuchâtel: Editions de la Baconnière, 1945.

Mercier, Vivian. *The New Novel from Queneau to Pinget*. New York: Farrar, Straus and Giroux, 1971.

Nadeau, Maurice. *Le Roman français depuis la guerre*. Paris: Gallimard, 1963.

Pouillon, Jean. "Règles du je." *Les Temps modernes,* 12:134 (April 1957), 1591–98.

_____. *Temps et roman*. Paris: Gallimard, 1946.

Ricardou, Jean. *Pour une Théorie du nouveau roman*. Paris: Seuil, Collection "Tel Quel," 1971.

_____. *Problèmes du nouveau roman*. Paris: Seuil, Collections "Tel Ouel," 1967.

Sarraute, Nathalie. *L'Ère du soupçon*. Paris: Gallimard, 1950.

Sturrock, John. *The French New Novel: Simon, Butor, Robbe-Grillet*. London: Oxford University Press, 1969.

Zants, Emily. *The Aesthetics of the New Novel in France*. Boulder, Colorado: Colorado University Press, 1968.

_____. "Relation of Epiphany to Description in the New Novel." *Comparative Literature Studies*, 1968.

Zeltner, Gerda. *La Grande Aventure du roman français au XXe siècle*. Paris: Editions Gonthier, 1967.

Zéraffa, Michel. *Personne et personnage: Le romanesque des années 1920 aux années 1950*. Paris: Editions Klincksieck, 1969.

## Special Numbers of Periodicals on the New Novel

*Esprit,* nouvelle série, "Le Nouveau Roman", nos. 7–8, July–August 1958.

*L'Esprit créateur,* vol. VII, no. 2, summer 1967.

*Modern Language Notes,* vol. 77, no. 3, May 1962.

*Revue des Lettres modernes,* nos. 94–99, "Un Nouveau Roman?" 1964.

*Yale French Studies,* no. 24, summer 1959.

### Sartre

Albérès, R. M. *Jean-Paul Sartre.* Paris: Editions Universitaires, 1953.

Cohn, Dorrit. "Narrated Monologue: Definition of a Fictional Style." *Comparative Literature,* 17:2 (spring 1966), 97–122.

Ehrmann, Jacques. "Of Rats and Men: Notes on the Prefaces." *Yale French Studies,* 30 (fall–winter, 1962–1963), 78–85.

Jameson, Fredric. *Sartre: The Origins of a Style.* New Haven: Yale University Press, 1961.

Koefoed, Oleg. "L'Oeuvre littéraire de Sartre." *Orbis Litterarum,* 6 (1948), 209–72 and 7 (1949), 61–141.

Sartre, Jean-Paul. "L'Enfance d'un chef." *Le Mur.* Paris: Gallimard, 1939.

—————. *Réflexions sur la question juive.* Paris: Gallimard, Collection Idées, 1954.

—————. *Situations I.* Paris: Gallimard, 1947.

—————. *Situations II.* Paris: Gallimard, 1948.

Smith, Madeleine. "The Making of a Leader." *Yale French Studies,* I (spring–summer 1948), 80–83.

Suhl, Benjamin. *Jean-Paul Sartre: The Philosopher as a Literary Critic.* New York and London: Columbia University Press, 1970.

Thody, Philip. *Jean-Paul Sartre: A Literary and Political Study.* London: Hamilton, 1960.

### Camus

Abbou, André. "Les paradoxes du discours dans *L'Étranger:* De la parole directe à l'écriture inverse." *Revue des lettres modernes,* nos. 212–16, *Langue et Langages,* 1969, 35–76.

Barrier, M.-G. *L'Art du récit dans* L'Étranger *d'Albert Camus.* Paris: A. G. Nizet, 1962.

Brée, Germaine, ed. *L'Étranger.* New York: Appleton-Century-Crofts, 1955.

Camus, Albert. *L'Étranger.* Paris: Bibliothèque de la Pléiade, NRF, 1962.

Castex, Pierre-Georges. *Albert Camus et "L'Étranger."* Paris: Corti, 1965.

Champigny, Robert. *Sur un héros païen.* Paris: "Les Essais," Gallimard, 1959.

Cruickshank, John. *Albert Camus and the Literature of Revolt.* London: Oxford University Press, 1959.

Fitch, Brian T. "Aspects de l'emploi du discours indirect libre dans *l'Étranger.*" *La Revue des lettres modernes,* 170–74, 1968.

――――――――. *Narrateur et narration dans* L'Étranger *d'Albert Camus.* Collection Archives des lettres modernes, no. 34. Paris: Minard, 1960. 2d ed. rev. and aug., 1968.

――――――――. *Le Sentiment d'étrangeté chez Malraux, Sartre, Camus et Simone de Beauvoir.* Bibliothèque des Lettres Modernes. Paris: Minard, 1964.

Gadourek, Carina. *Les Innocents et les coupables: Essai d'exégèse de l'oeuvre d'Albert Camus.* La Haye: Mouton, 1963.

Girard, René. "Camus's Stranger Retried." *PMLA,* 79:5 (December 1964), 519–33.

Pariente, J.-C. "L'Étranger et son double." *Revue des lettres modernes,* nos. 170–74, *Autour de* L'Étranger, 1968, 53–80.

*La Revue des lettres modernes,* special issues on Camus:
*Albert Camus I,* nos. 170–74, 1968 - 1.
*Albert Camus II,* nos. 212–16, 1969 - 5.
*Albert Camus III,* nos. 238–44, 1970 - 4.

*Symposium, Albert Camus,* 12:1-2 (1958).

――――――――. *Albert Camus II,* 24:3 (fall 1970).

Ullmann, Stephen. *The Image in the Modern French Novel.* Oxford: Blackwell, 1963.

Viggiani, Carl A. "Camus' 'L'Étranger.' " *PMLA,* 71:5 (December 1956), 865–87.

## Robbe-Grillet

Alter, Jean. *La Vision du monde d'Alain Robbe-Grillet.* Genève: Droz, 1966.

Anzieu, Didier. "Le Discours de l'obsessionel dans les romans de Robbe-Grillet." *Les Temps modernes,* 233 (1965), 608–37.

Barnes, Hazel E. "Modes of Aesthetic Consciousness in Fiction." *Bucknell Review,* 2:1 (March 1964), 82–93.

――――――――. "The Ins and Outs of Alain Robbe-Grillet." *Chicago Review,* 15:3 (winter–spring 1962), 21–40.

Bernal, Olga. *Alain Robbe-Grillet: Le Roman de l'absence.* Paris: Gallimard, 1964.

Brooke-Rose, Christine. "L'Imagination baroque de Robbe-Grillet," in J. H. Mathews, ed., *Un nouveau Roman? Recherches et traditions, Revue des Lettres modernes,* 1964.

Garzilli, Enrico. *Circles without Center.* Cambridge: Harvard University Press, 1972.

Lethcoe, James. "The Structure of Robbe-Grillet's Labyrinth." *French Review,* 38 (1965), 497–506.

Morrissette, Bruce. "De Stendhal à Robbe-Grillet: Modalités du 'point de vue.' " *Cahiers de l'Association Internationale des Études Françaises,* no. 14, June 1962.

――――――――. *Les Romans de Robbe-Grillet.* Paris: Editions de Minuit, 1964.

Pingaud, Bernard. *"Dans le Labyrinthe* d'Alain Robbe-Grillet." *Les Lettres nouvelles,* October 7, 1959, 38–41.

Porter, Dennis. "Sartre, Robbe-Grillet, and the Psychotic Hero." *Modern Fiction Studies,* 16:1 (spring 1970).

Robbe-Grillet. *Dans le Labyrinthe.* Paris: Editions de Minuit, 1959.

_____. *Pour un nouveau Roman.* Paris: Editions de Minuit, 1963.

Stoltzfus, Ben F. *Alain Robbe-Grillet and the New French Novel.* Carbondale: Southern Illinois University Press, 1964.